SOCIETY FOR NEW TESTAMENT STUDIES
MONOGRAPH SERIES

GENERAL EDITOR
MATTHEW BLACK, D.D., F.B.A.

7

JOHN THE BAPTIST
IN THE GOSPEL TRADITION

JOHN THE BAPTIST IN THE GOSPEL TRADITION

BY

WALTER WINK

Assistant Professor
Union Theological Seminary
New York

CAMBRIDGE
AT THE UNIVERSITY PRESS
1968

Published by the Syndics of the Cambridge University Press
Bentley House, 200 Euston Road, London, N.W. 1
American Branch: 32 East 57th Street, New York, N.Y. 10022

Library of Congress Catalogue Card Number: 68-21401

Standard Book Number: 521 07143 7

Printed in Great Britain
at the University Printing House, Cambridge
(Brooke Crutchley, University Printer)

CONTENTS

PREFACE

This study is a considerably modified version of my doctoral dissertation, *John the Baptist and the Gospel*, written under the New Testament Faculty at Union Theological Seminary in New York City. The serious student of the matters at hand is referred to that earlier work for a thorough treatment of the 'quest for the historical John' as it has developed from Reimarus to the present day, and for a detailed examination of John's relationship to the Community of Qumran. All of this material I have omitted for the sake of brevity.

My special thanks are extended to Dr W. D. Davies, Dr J. Louis Martyn, Dr John Knox, Dr James Muilenburg and Dr Cyril C. Richardson for their assistance to me in the course of my research; and to Dr William C. Robinson, Jr., of Perkins School of Theology, for his many helpful suggestions. To my wife, without whose encouragement and assistance this work could never have proceeded, this book is affectionately dedicated.

W. W.

Union Theological Seminary, New York
October 1967

LIST OF ABBREVIATIONS

AJT	*American Journal of Theology*
ATR	*Anglican Theological Review*
BZ	*Biblische Zeitschrift* (Neue Folge)
ET	*Expository Times*
GCS	*Die griechisch-christlichen Schriftsteller der ersten Jahrhunderte*
HTR	*Harvard Theological Review*
JBL	*Journal of Biblical Literature*
JTS	*Journal of Theological Studies*
NTS	*New Testament Studies*
PG	Migne, *Patrologia Graeca*
PL	Migne, *Patrologia Latina*
RGG	*Die Religion in Geschichte und Gegenwart*
RQ	*Revue de Qumran*
TWNT	*Theologisches Wörterbuch zum Neuen Testament*
ZNTW	*Zeitschrift für die neutestamentliche Wissenschaft*
ZThK	*Zeitschrift für Theologie und Kirche*

INTRODUCTION

For the past century and a half, the primary preoccupation of New Testament research has been the quest for the historical Jesus. In this quest John the Baptist has attracted considerable attention, for while there are no reliable non-Christian witnesses to the life of Jesus, there is valuable mention of John the Baptist in the writings of Josephus. The history of John the Baptist has therefore served as the seemingly secure bedrock on which the reconstruction of the history of Jesus could proceed. To be sure, the source-material which deals with John is exceedingly sketchy, but it has been considered sufficient to serve as the basis for volume after volume of 'Lives of John'. All of this research has culminated in a rather broad consensus among scholars today on the main issues of the life of John the Baptist, and even those points which still remain problematical have been brought to within the range of but a few possibilities.[1]

---

[1] For a thorough discussion of the historical problems the reader is referred to the leading monographs on John the Baptist. The work of Martin Dibelius, *Die urchristliche Überlieferung von Johannes dem Täufer* [henceforth *Johannes der Täufer*] (1911), provides an indispensible form-critical prolegomenon to any study of John. Building on this pioneering analysis are the three most prominent monographs: Maurice Goguel's *Au seuil de l'évangile Jean-Baptiste* [henceforth *Jean-Baptiste*] (1928); Ernst Lohmeyer's *Das Urchristentum I. Johannes der Täufer* [henceforth *Johannes der Täufer*] (1932); and above all, Carl H. Kraeling's *John the Baptist* (1951). More recently we have the works of Jean Steinmann, *John the Baptist and the Desert Tradition*, tr. by Michael Boyes (1958); Charles H. H. Scobie, *John the Baptist* (1964); David Flusser, *Johannes der Täufer* (1964); and Roland Schütz, *Johannes der Täufer* (*Abhandlungen zur Theologie des Alten und Neuen Testaments*, Band 50) (1967).

Also of major importance are the relevant sections of David Friedrich Strauss' *Life of Jesus* (tr. by George Eliot from the 4th German ed. of 1840); Albert Schweitzer's *Quest of the Historical Jesus* (tr. by W. Montgomery from the first German ed. of 1906); Gunther Bornkamm's *Jesus of Nazareth*, tr. by I. and F. McLuskey (1960), pp. 44–52; Philipp Vielhauer's 'Johannes der Täufer', *RGG*³ (1959), III, 803–7; and, for a divergent view, William R. Farmer's 'John the Baptist', *Interpreter's Dictionary of the Bible* (1962), II, 955–62. For other references see notes and bibliography.

Except for these points, this corner, at least, of the quest for the historical Jesus would seem to have been secured.

In other sectors, however, the Jesus-quest was faring badly. The attempt to establish the historicity of the Gospel accounts was constantly foundering on the relative unconcern of the Gospels for historicity as such. The Evangelists were not interested in scientific history, but salvation. They wrote, not to preserve accurate records, but to create and to edify believers. Indeed, when the individual units of the Gospel tradition were analyzed according to the history of their transmission (form criticism), it became clear that scarcely a word of the Gospels is uncolored by the faith of the church. In the face of these discoveries it became problematic whether a quest for the historical Jesus was possible at all.

Yet, ironically, while the quest for the historical Jesus had its messengers of defeat, the quest for the historical John had none. The very success of the John-quest led to its fixation on the level of historicity. Every monograph on John which has thus far appeared has dealt with him from the point of view of historical biography. Scholars have consistently regarded the early church's *theological* preoccupation with John as simply so much pious legend, as mythological or devotional husk to be stripped off in the search for the bare kernels of historical fact. And it is not our contention that historical facts cannot be established concerning the life of John. What we do argue, however, is that when the bare facts about John are known, they nevertheless fail to answer the very questions about him which we *must* have answered in order to make sense of the New Testament record. Why is John the Baptist accorded such a prominent place in the Gospel tradition? Why, for that matter, is he mentioned at all? Why did Jesus lavish on John words of such high praise that the church would later find them a source of profound embarrassment? And why, in spite of this, did the church include John in the Christian proclamation, and assert what they could have left unsaid: that John marked the turning point in the history of salvation?

These are the questions the historian wishes to have answered, yet it is precisely these questions which have largely been neglected.[1] Such questions should make it clear to one at all familiar with the subject that the Gospels are no more concerned about the 'history' of John than they are about the 'history' of Jesus. John, too, is regarded by the Evangelists primarily from a theological point of view. Scholars have succeeded rather well in isolating the historical facts about John, they have evaluated his stature as a man and his influence upon Jesus, but they have not explained why the church made him the first preacher of the 'good news' (Mark 1: 1-4 par.; Luke 3: 18; cf. 1: 19); or why, at extreme risk to the uniqueness of Jesus, the shapers of the earliest traditions drew John up into the Christian *kerygma* (Acts 10: 37; 13: 24; and of course the Gospels themselves), and declared that it was with *his* coming that the Gospel could be said to 'begin' (Mark 1: 1; Luke 1: 5 ff.; 3: 1 ff.; 16: 16; Matt. 3: 2; 11: 12 f.; John 1: 6, 19 ff.).

What is the source of the church's intense interest in John? The reason which scholars have generally advanced is that the early church found itself in continuing competition with John's disciples, and that as an evangelistic stratagem the church absorbed John into the Gospel message, making John a witness against his own disciples to the messiahship of Jesus. This hypothesis will be given careful consideration in the study which follows, for it has never been seriously tested. But even if, as we shall see, the church did on occasion find itself polemically engaged with John's disciples, is it valid to generalize from these localized instances and interpret the entire body of tradition about John as polemically inspired? Has the church adopted John in order to use him against his own disciples, or could it use him against his disciples (as occasion demanded) because he was already a part of the Gospel message? And how shall we explain the quite exalted religious value attached to John in passages which betray no polemical or apologetical tendencies whatever?

If the methodological impasse in the study of John the Baptist has resulted from the failure to take seriously the original

[1] Cf. for instance the revealing comment by Charles H. H. Scobie, *op. cit.* p. 11: 'What this book attempts to do is precisely what the Gospels do not do: to investigate the life of John for its own sake.'

intention of the creators of the Gospel accounts, then the logical procedure would be to examine the manner in which each Evangelist has used the traditions about John in proclaiming the good news of Jesus Christ. For it would appear that the real significance of John—even his proper historical significance, in so far as it can be measured by his impact on others—can best be discovered by asking the question concerning John in the same way that it was asked by the early church: what is the role of John the Baptist in God's redemptive purpose? That is to say, what is the role of John the Baptist in the Gospels and Acts?

CHAPTER I

JOHN THE BAPTIST IN THE GOSPEL OF MARK

It will be our task in the chapters that follow to discover the significance of John the Baptist for the writers of the Gospels and Acts. Such an investigation assumes that the individual Evangelist has left his mark upon the material he has edited, and that by analyzing the redactor's treatment and placing of the material we can decipher his theological and religious presuppositions. This form of inquiry has been labeled *Redaktionsgeschichte* ('the history of redaction', or 'redaction-criticism'). In regarding the Evangelist seriously, 'redaction-criticism' does not repudiate the principles of form criticism but rather *extends* them to the study of the Gospel form itself.[1] We begin therefore with the creator of the Gospel form—Mark.

A. THE INTRODUCTION (Mark 1: 1–15)

Mark's opening thrust is amazingly compressed. It covers the period from John's appearance to the beginning of Jesus' ministry in such a way that the whole complex of events is a single movement, the beginning of the Gospel. Marxsen[2] rightly insists that the entire Gospel of Mark is to be understood from the end backward; it is the resurrection which has made meaningful the passion, it is the passion which has given new significance to the healings, exorcisms and parables, it is the ministry which points to Jesus' baptism as its source. Likewise every detail in the introductory narrative points backward. Jesus' baptism (1: 9–11) points back to John's prophecy of the messiah's coming and the baptism of the Holy Spirit (1: 4–8), and John's coming points back to the Old Testament prophecies which anticipated the future salvation (1: 2–3). Therefore

---

[1] W. Marxsen, *Der Evangelist Markus* (1956), p. 11. E. Haenchen prefers to call this approach *Kompositionsgeschichte* ('the history of composition') (*Der Weg Jesu: Eine Erklärung des Markus-Evangeliums und der kanonischen Parallelen*, 1966, p. 24). [2] *Ibid.* pp. 17–19.

Mark 1 : 1 stands not only as an introduction to the subject but even more as a summary of its entire content: in all these events —Old Testament prophecies, John's mission, the baptism of Jesus—we see the beginning of the good news of Jesus Christ.

Thus Mark makes it clear from the outset that the Baptist traditions are entirely subservient to the Jesus traditions. John has no significance in himself, for all the statements about him are in reality Christological ones.[1] When Mark begins to tell us who John is he does so in terms of a composite quotation from Mal. 3: 1; Exod. 23: 20 and Isa. 40: 3, passages which evoke the image of the forerunner Elijah (Mal. 4: 5).[2] Mark tells us almost nothing of John's preaching or activity. Instead he mentions John's diet and clothing (1 : 6). Why such unimportant details? Because they build progressively to a confirmation of John's role

[1] Marxsen, *Der Evangelist Markus*, p. 19. Mark is no more concerned with pure historicity in his presentation of John than is the Fourth Evangelist (Ernst Lohmeyer, 'Zur evangelischen Überlieferung von Johannes der Täufer', *JBL*, LI, 1932, 302 f.), though he is more restrained.

[2] J. A. T. Robinson ('Elijah, John and Jesus: An Essay in Detection', *NTS*, IV, 1957–8, 267; republished in *Twelve New Testament Studies*, 1962, p. 34) argues that Mark 1: 2 has been interpolated into Mark under the influence of Matt. 11: 10 and Luke 7: 27. It is clear from an examination of the parallels that Mark 1: 2 is far closer in form to its synoptic sisters than to either Mal. 3: 1 or Exod. 23: 20. Note that (a) neither Matthew nor Luke employs the Malachi citation in the baptism account even though they use the Isa. 40: 3 citation which follows; it is possible that their copies of Mark lacked the reference to Malachi; (b) Mark had introduced the quotations by 'as it is written in *Isaiah* the prophet'; had there been any question as to the pedigree of his quotation he could have quite truthfully said merely 'as it is written'.

On the other hand, Mark is extremely lax about Scripture citations (e.g. 1 : 11; 9: 12). If he received this scriptural conglomerate already fused in this manner he may well have thought the whole thing came from Isaiah. The fact that his form is close to that of Matt. 11: 10 par. suggests that all three Evangelists received the passage through the mediation of Christian 'testimony' collections, for the Matthean form must also be accounted for. The Old Testament passages are so similar that confusion is not surprising; Adolf Schlatter even suggests that Mal. 3: 1 itself is based on Isa. 40: 3 (*Johannes der Täufer*, 1956 [1880], p. 17)! Debarim Rabbah connects the messenger of Malachi with the prediction in Isa. 40: 4 (cf. E. A. Abbott, *From Letter to Spirit*, 1903, p. 211 n. 4); apparently others felt free to combine these quite similar prophecies (cf. also Exodus Rabbah 23: 20). The most decisive arguments in favor of the text as it stands, however, are that Mark 1: 2 fits into Mark's conception and purpose perfectly, and that there is absolutely no textual evidence that a copy of Mark ever existed without v. 2.

as forerunner. His clothing is like that of the prophet Elijah (II Kings 1: 8; Zech. 13: 4),[1] his diet that of the strict Nazarites of old. 'All' the people hear him and repent. The perceptive reader cannot miss Mark's point: John is the prophet of the end-time, the eschatological messenger of Malachi; yes, he is Elijah who is to 'come first to restore *all* things' (Mark 9: 11). The allusion is to Mal. 4: 5 f., which states that Elijah will come just before the end to 'restore [LXX—ἀποκαταστήσει] the hearts of the fathers to their children', etc. In Judaism this restoration came to be conceived of as a mass repentance on the part of all Israel.[2] If 'all' have now repented at the word of John, is he not Elijah who is to come?[3]

Mark's purpose is therefore clarified on the basis of 9: 11. John is 'the *beginning* of the good news of Jesus Christ' because

[1] C. K. Barrett (*The Gospel According to St John*, 1960, p. 144) prefers as the original reading of Mark 1: 6 the variant in D and the Italian family of MSS, which omit 'and had a leather girdle around his waist'. Barrett's reasoning is that this addition identifies John with Elijah and is therefore secondary. But the text of D is notoriously corrupt in Mark 1, and allusions to Elijah are already present elsewhere in Mark 1: 1–8.

[2] One can virtually speak of a Jewish 'doctrine' of the necessity for a final repentance. 'If you [plural] keep the Law, expect Elijah (Mal. 3: 24)' (Sifre Deut. 41). 'Israel will fulfil the great repentance when Elijah of blessed memory comes, as it is said (Mal. 3: 24)' (Pirqe R. Eliezer 43 [25a]). These references rest on early traditions. (Cf. Strack–Billerbeck, *Kommentar zum NT*, 1928, I, 598; C. Montefiore, 'Rabbinic Conceptions of Repentance', *Jewish Quarterly Review*, XVI, 1903–4, 209–57; G. F. Moore, *Judaism*, 1932, I, 520 ff.)

[3] Mark possibly has in mind the same 'scribal' conception of Elijah (9: 11) as Trypho in Justin's *Dial. cum Trypho* 8, 4 (cf. 49, 1): 'The Christ—if he has indeed been born and exists anywhere—is unknown and does not even know himself, and has no power, until Elias comes to anoint him and make him known to all.' The Mekilta on Exod. 16: 33 reflects a view parallel to that of Trypho in which Elijah is to restore three things: the jar of manna, the flask of water of lustration, and the flask of anointing oil (G. F. Moore, *Judaism*, II, 359 f.).

The idea of an unknown Messiah was certainly current in various forms in the first century. It is presupposed by the question John is said to have asked from prison (Matt. 11: 2/Luke 7: 19), and is openly stated in John 7: 27 ('when the Christ appears, no one will know where he comes from'). And in Acts 10: 38 the baptism of Jesus is described as an anointing with the Holy Spirit.

With some of these conceptions in mind Mark may have reduced the description of John in 1: 1–8 to but a hint of his identity as Elijah. Then in 1: 9–11 John anoints Jesus, who is hitherto unknown and perhaps even unaware of his calling.

3

Elijah must 'come *first* to restore all things'. Therefore not what he says or does matters so much as what he *is*. The very fact of his appearance is an eschatological event of the first magnitude, and can only mean one thing: the end is at hand. Thus Mark reduces John's message to but two sentences, both of which *anticipate* something to come. The statement is unmistakably clear: John is the forerunner of the messiah (1: 7), and his baptism a preparation for the messianic baptism to come (1: 8).[1]

Just as Jesus' advent is marked by the citation of Isa. 42: 1 (Mark 1: 11), so the advent of John is explained by Scripture. From the point of view of transition 1: 4 is tied to 1: 3 by means of the identical phrase ἐν τῇ ἐρήμῳ in both verses. Marxsen goes to great pains to prove that this phrase was not in the tradition which Mark received and that he added it to conform John to the image required by Isa. 40: 3.[2] The point of objection upon which Marxsen fastens is that 'Jordan' and 'wilderness' are incompatible. Luke certainly feels this to be true, for he separates the two areas; John leaves the wilderness and goes to the Jordan region after his call (Luke 3: 2 f.), just as Jesus later 'returned from the Jordan' and entered the wilderness to be tempted (4: 1). But Luke knows nothing about the Jordan region. He assumes, as have many scholars since, that river valleys are fertile and therefore cannot be designated 'wilderness' or 'desert'. The Jordan valley, however, is an exception. R. W. Funk has demonstrated conclusively that the lower Jordan valley was called 'desert' in both the Old and New Testament periods, ἔρημος being used in the latter for both מדבר and ערבה (cf. Isa. 40: 3, where the two Hebrew terms are used synonymously).[3] In Matt. 11: 7 Jesus asks concerning

[1] Mark retains no trace of John's preaching of judgement. Even the reference to baptism 'in fire' is lacking from 1: 8. John's message is viewed completely from the point of view of the redemption experienced in Jesus Christ; the judgement now awaits the *parousia* (Mark 13: 27).

[2] Marxsen, *Der Evangelist Markus*, pp. 20–2, 26–9, following K. L. Schmidt, *Der Rahmen der Geschichte Jesus* (1919), pp. 18 ff. The suggestion was put forward earlier by W. Brandt, *Die jüdischen Baptismen* (1910), p. 71. Cf. also R. Bultmann, *The History of the Synoptic Tradition*, translated by John Marsh (1963), p. 246, who, however, concedes that 1: 4 and 6 'are not editorial in character' and probably already lay in the pre-Markan tradition.

[3] 'The Wilderness', *JBL*, LXXVIII (1959), 205–14; cf. also C. C. McCown, 'The Scene of John's Ministry', *JBL*, LIX (1940), 113–31; W. H. Brownlee,

John, 'What did you go out *into the wilderness* to behold? A *reed* shaken by the wind?' Reeds (κάλαμοι) grow only along river banks. Or again, in John 11 : 54 the town Ephraim is said to be 'near the wilderness'. Ephraim was probably four miles north-east of Bethel on the site of the modern village ẹt-Ṭaiyibeh, on the crest of the western slopes of the Jordan River cleft ten miles north-west of Jericho. The 'wilderness' and the Jordan region are identical.

It would be more accurate to say, then, that Mark *preserved* the wilderness tradition which he found in his sources because it suited his theological purpose, or better, that his theological purpose was itself *created* by this element in the tradition. Because John *was* 'in the wilderness' the Isaiah citation becomes relevant. In at least this case the historical tradition has determined the course which the scriptural proof-from-prophecy has taken, and not the reverse.

Just as John provides the *Vorgeschichte* for Jesus, so also there is a *Vorgeschichte* behind John: the Old Testament. This is apparently the meaning of 1 : 2–3. The 'beginning' is not just the point of departure for Mark's Gospel but even more the earliest point back to which present facts can be traced in order to display their meaning.[1] The events clustered around the beginning thus stand under the formula 'as it is written', a phrase common to almost all *kerygmatic* recitals in the New Testament. With a single citation the whole Old Testament is called to bear witness to the Gospel which has at last broken into the world. The entire Gospel of Mark is thereby an extended *kerygma*. Resurrection, death, suffering, ministry all lead back to the forerunner, and through John even the Old Testament prophecies become a part of the 'beginning of the Gospel of Jesus Christ'.

James M. Robinson notes that while the 'beginning of the gospel' is announced in *v.* 1, the 'preaching of the gospel' is mentioned only in *vv.* 14–15, when John is already in prison. It is further remarkable that the good news is introduced (*v.* 2) by a prophecy of what *will* happen: κατασκευάσει, whereas the

'John the Baptist', in *The Scrolls and the New Testament*, ed. K. Stendahl (1957), p. 34; and in regard to Luke's geographical references, Hans Conzelmann, *The Theology of St Luke*, tr. by G. Buswell (1960), pp. 18 f.

[1] Marxsen, *Der Evangelist Markus*, pp. 24 f.

good news as summarized on Jesus' lips consists of an announcement of what *has* happened: πεπλήρωται, ἤγγικεν. Robinson concludes that the shift of tenses indicates that 'the times have shifted, the kingdom is now near because it has moved from a vague distance to a near position'.[1] This shift, be it noted, is not between the time of John and that of Jesus, but between the time of prophecy (Old Testament) and that of fulfilment (John the Baptist). It is with John that the gospel 'begins'.[2]

Yet at the same time John does not fully belong to the time of fulfilment, for his message as recorded by Mark is entirely prophetic. John is distinguished from the time of the Old Testament in terms of fulfilment (1 : 2 ff.) but from that of Jesus in terms of anticipation (1 : 7 f.). The messenger of victory is not the victor. The deliberate manner in which Mark has distinguished John's ministry both from previous Judaism (1 : 1 ff.) and from the ministry of Jesus (1 : 14 ff.) indicates that he is working with a clear conception of John's significance. Yet Mark has not invented this distinction; it is so pervasive in our sources that we must conclude that it was already of some theological importance to the early church.[3] The distinction of John from Judaism is attested to in Acts 1 : 22; Matt. 11 : 7–10 (Q); Luke 1; 3 : 1 f.; Matt. 3 : 2; Ign. Smyr. 1 : 1; etc.; the distinction of the ministry of John from that of Jesus is evident in Acts 10 : 37 and Luke 3 : 1–20, which take their lead from Mark, and in Mark 2 : 18 f.; Matt. 11 : 2–6, 11 *b* (Q); 3 : 14 f. Both motifs appear side by side in Acts 13 : 24 f.; 19 : 3 f.; and Matt. 11 : 11. This dual distinction stands in its simplest form in Mark. By setting John's ministry apart from both the period of the Old Testament and the ministry of Jesus, Mark reveals John's function. He is the prophesied (1 : 2 f.) preparer of Jesus' way (1 : 9–13).[4] Yet, despite the distinction of their functions, all

---

[1] *The Problem of History in Mark* (1957), pp. 23 f.

[2] Robinson observes that the good news begins to happen (*v.* 4, John preaches a baptism of repentance for the forgiveness of sins) before it begins to be proclaimed as such (1 : 14 f.). This fact indicates that the content of the gospel is not 'some abstract, non-historical truth which, by being eternal, has no beginning save the beginning equal to its discovery or proclamation'; rather the gospel consists of a total event which can begin to happen even before it is proclaimed to have begun (*ibid.*).

[3] *Ibid.* p. 22.

[4] *Ibid.* pp. 22 f.

three—Old Testament, John and Jesus—participate in the event called by Mark 'the beginning of the gospel'.

What then does Mark mean by the term 'gospel'? Marxsen has shown that the term 'gospel' is not common to the synoptic traditions but has been introduced by Mark.[1] In Mark 8: 35 and 10: 29 Mark uses the phrase 'for my sake and for the gospel'. In both contexts Mark is speaking to the situation of the persecuted Roman church;[2] he who suffers for the gospel also suffers for Christ. Apparently Mark distinguishes between Jesus and the gospel here, yet in 1: 1 the gospel *is* Jesus Christ. Marxsen concludes from this that Jesus is both the content and the bringer of the gospel, that the gospel does not simply preach *about* Jesus but rather it preaches Jesus; that is, not Jesus' teachings but Jesus himself as Son of God is preached, and in such a way that Jesus himself is made present. Thus Marxsen can say that Jesus is God's good news.[3] But Marxsen fails to account adequately for the distinction implied by 'for my sake and for the gospel' and for the fact that both John and the Old Testament prophecies are gathered up into the gospel in 1: 1 ff. If, as Marxsen himself has shown, 'gospel' in 1: 1 summarizes Mark's whole message, then the gospel must be given a comprehensive definition. It is *the whole of God's saving activity as seen from the point of view of its fulfilment in the event of Jesus Christ.*[4] Behind the ministries of Jesus, John, even the Old Testament, lies the saving purpose of God.

Yet Mark scarcely does justice to Israel's rich heritage of prophecy by his brief citation in 1: 2 f. He makes no attempt to relate this good news to the history of Israel. Instead the Old Testament is simply gathered into the present act of salvation

---

[1] *Der Evangelist Markus*, pp. 77–83. This is especially true at 1: 1 and 1: 14 f. At 8: 35, 10: 29 and 13: 9 f. Mark has added a reference to 'the gospel' where his source had only 'for my sake'. Mark 14: 9 is problematic but the word 'gospel' here also is likely to be Mark's doing. Apparently Matthew finds εὐαγγέλιον only in Mark, never in his sources. Luke uses the verb but never the noun. Mark probably adapted the term from early Christian preaching as the key word to describe that preaching.

[2] This is clearest in 8: 34, where Mark has '*the multitude* with his disciples', i.e. the obligation to take up one's cross is applicable to all Christians, not just church leaders.   [3] *Ibid.* pp. 85–9.

[4] Thus Jesus preaches the gospel of *God* (1: 14). Cf. the way in which event and person are related by John Knox in *Jesus, Lord and Christ* (1958), pp. 193–276. The 'event of Jesus Christ' here includes John.

by the slightest reference, but a reference which makes abundantly clear the meaning of these present acts. For Mark is completely preoccupied with Jesus and with the future. His view is prospective rather than retrospective.[1] Therefore he can begin *in medias res* without an account of either the birth or the preparation of Jesus. He is content to say merely that into a world which knew no good news the good news of Jesus Christ has now come.

Mark does have a view of history, however. T. A. Burkill finds four periods in the historical realization of God's plan of salvation:

(1) The period of preparation—until John's removal to prison.

(2) The period of Jesus' ministry on earth, characterized by suffering and obscurity.

(3) The period after the resurrection, in which the gospel of the Christ is openly proclaimed.

(4) The period of eschatological fulfilment, gloriously inaugurated by the Son of man at his still-awaited parousia.[2]

This schematism admittedly is oversimplified, yet it is basically correct. The openness of the first period indicates its provisional character. Later Evangelists were to fix its limits more precisely. It should be noted, however, that it is Jesus Christ who gives unity and meaning to the entire scheme. These periods are not epochs of world history; they are rather but episodes in the manifestation of Jesus Christ to the world. There are only two real epochs, B.C. and A.D.[3]

B. THE IMPRISONMENT AND DEATH OF THE BAPTIST
(Mark 1: 14; 6: 14–29)

'Now after John was arrested, Jesus came into Galilee, preaching the gospel of God' (1: 14). According to Marxsen, an impression of successiveness has been deliberately created here by Mark where none existed before. Why else would he interject the report of John's arrest at 1: 14 and yet delay the account of

---

[1] T. A. Burkill, 'St Mark's Philosophy of History', *NTS*, III, 2 (1956–7), 145.　　[2] *Ibid.* pp. 142 f.

[3] Cf. Cullmann's discussion, *Christ and Time*, tr. by F. Filson (1950), pp. 17 ff. Mark's view of history falls short of a developed *Heilsgeschichte* since it fails to deal seriously with the epoch 'B.C.'.

his death till 6: 14 ff.? Since παραδοθῆναι ('to be delivered up, arrested') is used in 1: 14 in the absolute sense, just as elsewhere it is used by Mark only of Jesus, Marxsen thinks Mark is creating a parallelism between the two men. Historically, John's arrest belongs later; theologically it belongs here as a foretaste of the passion, just as chapters 1–13 contain foretastes of the cross. The complex dealing with the Baptist is thereby separated and set before the complex concerning Jesus. Mark 1: 14 is thus, in Schmidt's phrase, an 'unchronologische Chronologie' set in a 'heilsgeschichtliche Schematismus'.[1]

Here again Marxsen errs by mistaking the manner in which Mark goes about constructing theology. The work of Vincent Taylor,[2] W. L. Knox[3] and M. Albertz[4] has demonstrated how restrained Mark is with his sources, sometimes including whole blocks without substantial change (e.g. 2: 1–3: 6). Mark makes his point in the way that he *uses* his material as much as in the way that he changes it. Therefore the point is not unimportant: does Mark 'invent' the impression of successiveness, or does he find it already in the tradition? Does he have a prior conception of successiveness which he forces upon the traditions, or is Mark's view itself formed by the traditions?

Mark 6: 14 shows conclusively that the activities of Jesus and John were both chronologically and spatially separated. Jesus is taken for John the Baptist raised from the dead. Those who expressed this opinion could not have seen the two of them working together, or known of Jesus' baptism by John or even of a period of Jesus' discipleship under John. So long as John was baptizing and preaching, at least a part of the people must not have noticed Jesus. This does not exclude the possibility that Jesus was at first more or less a disciple of John; it means only that the public activity which brought him to the notice of the populace could only have begun after John was removed from the scene, i.e. arrested (1: 14). The people have an impression of successiveness, not contemporaneousness.[5]

[1] Marxsen, *Der Evangelist Markus*, pp. 22–4.
[2] *The Gospel According to St Mark* (1952).
[3] *The Sources of the Synoptic Gospels*, vol. 1 (1953).
[4] *Die synoptischen Streitgespräche* (1921).
[5] Cullmann, *The Christology of the New Testament*, tr. by S. C. Guthrie and C. A. M. Hall (1959), pp. 31 f. Cf. also A. Schweitzer, *The Quest of the Historical Jesus*, p. 373; and Bultmann, *The History of the Synoptic Tradition*,

John is dead. Jesus appears, and his behavior so strikingly resembles John's that people leap to the conclusion that he is John risen from the dead. The belief expressed here is not that John has been resurrected (ἀνάστασις) but that he has been physically resuscitated (ἐγήγερται—6: 14): raised from the grave, not brought back from heaven (as, i.e., Elijah, who never died).[1] We find here not a confession of faith in God's vindication of John by his resurrection, but rather a crude popular superstition, a reaction of hope, fear, or, in Herod's case, guilt. This superstition presupposes, however, that Jesus was unknown to the opponents of John until after John's death.[2]

The fact that this successiveness is historical does not mean that Mark 1: 14 or 6: 17 ff. are strictly chronological. But it does mean that Mark is doing his best to reconstruct the chronological relationship between Jesus and John which the tradition implies. John's role as forerunner can be emphasized by Mark in 1: 14 precisely because he actually did 'run before', and had been imprisoned before Jesus' public ministry began.

What is really significant is not the chronology implied by a passage like 6: 14–29, but the fact that this rambling, unedifying account of John's death is included at all.[3] After telescoping

p. 302 n. 1: '...the conclusion follows, that in contrast to the presentation in John, the ministry of Jesus did not begin until after the death of John the Baptist.'

[1] So Cullmann, *Christology*, p. 33, following E. Lichtenstein, 'Die älteste christliche Glaubensformel', *Zeitschrift für Kirchengeschichte*, LXIII (1950), 26 ff.

[2] Matt. 11: 2–6 rests on the memory that Jesus' public ministry burgeoned only after John was in prison—why else would Jesus need to tell John what he has done? Acts 13: 24 f. makes it clear that Jesus only began to call his disciples shortly before John's arrest: 'and as John *was finishing his course*...' And in Mark 8: 28 Jesus is again taken as the resuscitated John, an opinion which could only arise if Jesus was comparatively unknown during John's ministry.

On the other hand, John 3: 22 ff. may indicate that there was a period during which Jesus baptized contemporaneously with John (cf. C. H. Dodd, *Historical Tradition in the Fourth Gospel*, 1963, pp. 285–301). If this was the case, however, the period of their joint activity was so brief (John 4: 1–3) that even in the Fourth Gospel the impression of successiveness prevails (cf. John 1: 15, 30; 10: 40 ff.).

[3] Note how drastically Matthew and Luke condense it. W. L. Knox, *The Sources of the Synoptic Gospels*, I, 50, demonstrates the popular character of 6: 17–29. He calls it, following Rawlinson, a 'bazaar rumour', and

the entire ministry of John into four verses in chapter one, Mark's leisurely narrative here is somewhat disconcerting. No doubt Mark is fascinated by the gory story. But he has a point to make. He places it after the report of Jesus' increasing popularity and success, and tells us how the report reacted on Herod's guilt for having killed John. Herod, more superstitious than even the rabble, fears that John has come back to haunt him (6: 16). It thus becomes necessary at this point to narrate John's death, even though *vv.* 14–16 assume that John has already been dead for some time. Mark apparently intends to draw a parallel between John and Jesus and to indicate that Jesus at this point was in the same kind of danger that had formerly proved fatal to John.[1] But Mark fails to develop this lead; instead of picturing Jesus' withdrawal after John's death as a flight from Herod (as does Matt. 14: 13), Mark makes it a rest-retreat (6: 31). Apparently the necessity to ward off charges of political sedition has intervened, so that he offers the merest suggestion that Jesus faces the fate of John.

Likewise there is no indication that the account of John's death is intended to serve a polemical purpose. Dibelius concluded from the belief that John had been resuscitated (6: 14–16; 8: 28) that the people refused to believe in the death of their hero. Mark's report of the death of John is so stark in its details, and the notice that John's disciples buried his body is so final, that one might conclude that Mark was seeking to counteract just such a belief.[2] If this were the case, however, Mark surely would have suppressed 6: 14–16 and 8: 28, since they lend credence to the belief in John's resuscitation. Yet our only sources for the belief that John was resuscitated are these very verses in Mark. Therefore we must conclude that no polemic is intended.

Nor do we find evidence of polemic against the disciples of John elsewhere in Mark's Gospel. Mark 1: 7 reads '*stoop down and untie*', a phrase not paralleled by any of the other evangelists. But it is uncertain whether Mark has added it or whether

adds: 'nor does it even profess to come from the disciples of John.' The inaccuracies in the narrative are patent (cf. Maurice Goguel, *Jean-Baptiste*, p. 53 n. 3).

[1] T. W. Manson, *The Servant Messiah* (1956), pp. 40 f. Cf. also Ernest Best, *The Temptation and the Passion: The Markan Soteriology* (1965), p. 135: '...John's Passion is an indication of the Passion of Jesus.'

[2] Martin Dibelius, *Johannes der Täufer*, pp. 85 f.

it is one of the vivid, irrelevant details brought in by his sources. In any case its presence indicates no special desire to subordinate John since the act of untying sandals necessarily involves stooping down.[1] Again, in Mark 2: 18–19 Jesus is criticized because his disciples (many of whom in all probability had been disciples of John) do not fast as do John's disciples. The implication is that hitherto Jesus and his disciples have been considered a part of John's movement; now the divergences are beginning to appear (cf. Matt. 11: 16–19). But in the course of transmission, two additions to the passage have completely transformed its meaning. First, 2: 20 was added, indicating that the church regarded the interim until the return of Christ as a time for fasting, and was seeking by means of this interpolation to justify current practice. By this change, however, the radical difference between John's pre-messianic travail and Jesus' messianic feast is lost, and the distinction between their movements dissolves. Secondly, the phrase 'and the Pharisees' was added in order to transform the saying into a contrast between Judaism and Christianity; to this the logion on new patches and new wine was attached.[2] Apparently then the original context was no longer

[1] There is no justification for Bultmann's assertion (*The History of the Synoptic Tradition*, pp. 246 f.) that the saying about the 'mightier one' in Mark 1: 7 is a Christian addition reflecting the rivalry between the church and John's disciples. His misconception of the relationship between the two groups is dealt with below (pp. 98–110).

[2] Cf. V. Taylor, *The Gospel According to St Mark* (1952), pp. 208–12. Bultmann regards 19a as a secular mashal used by the church at a time when conflict with the Baptist sect was acute. Since it is the conduct of the disciples which is questioned, and Jesus defends their action, not his own, Bultmann feels that the church is appealing to Jesus in defense of its practice (*The History of the Synoptic Tradition*, pp. 18 f.). But what authority would an appeal to Jesus have against Baptists? And why would the church owe Baptists any defense of its actions? Had the church invented the setting, we would have expected a construction similar to Matt. 3: 14 or Luke 3: 15, with appeal made to *John* against the practices of his own disciples, such as: 'and John said to his disciples, "Can the wedding guests fast while the bridegroom is with them?"' Cf. also John 3: 28. On p. 105, however, Bultmann reckons with the possibility that the mashal in Mark 2: 19a was originally applied to himself by Jesus.

E. Percy, *Die Botschaft Jesu* (1953), p. 234, holds that 2: 18–20 is essentially authentic, since the church regarded the messianic wedding feast as a future hope (Rev. 19: 7 ff.; Matt. 25: 1–13), and the passage grimly anticipates a time of sorrow without reference to the resurrection.

relevant. We may conclude from this that nowhere in the later course of development of 2: 18–20 was there any awareness of conflict with a Baptist movement.

Nor does Mark reflect conflict with Baptists elsewhere. Had he been aware of such conflict he would surely not have subordinated Jesus to John at the baptism (1: 9–11), nor pictured Jesus as John's successor (1: 14 f.), nor allowed the opinion to drop from Herod's lips that Jesus is just John returned to haunt him (6: 16). Nor would Mark have spoken of John's 'powers' (6: 14), nor allowed Jesus to stake his own authority entirely on that of John (11: 30–2). It is not for polemical purposes, then, that Mark has included the account of John's death.

At the center of 6: 14–29, therefore, stands not a warning to Jesus nor anti-Baptist polemic, but simply the suffering of John. Yet he is not portrayed as a martyr. Nothing is said of his courage in the face of suffering or of his unswerving faith in the final triumph of his cause. In fact he scarcely manages to appear in his own death-scene at all! The emphasis is rather on what *they* do to him.[1] Apparently John's suffering is of such importance to Mark that he is willing to include this entire episode just to make this single point. What Mark understands by this enigmatic suffering-scene is revealed in 9: 9–13.

C. ELIJAH SUFFERS (Mark 9: 9–13)

This passage teems with confusion. Mark phrases *v.* 10 in such a manner that the disciples appear to be ignorant about the general resurrection. In *v.* 12 he completely loses track of the point about Elijah when he stumbles across the saying on the suffering of the Son of man, so that he has to complete the first idea in *v.* 13. Twice he cites scriptures which are nonexistent; this is especially bewildering since Mark is so little concerned with proof-from-prophecy elsewhere. Most puzzling of all is that Mark never really tells us what he means. Why does he not go on and say what we all know, that John is Elijah?

Mark has not created all of these problems; some of them already lay in the tradition. The idea that Elijah must first come

---

[1] It is possible that Herod and Herodias are intended to evoke the picture of Ahab and Jezebel arrayed against Elijah, but this is uncertain.

is certainly scriptural,[1] but Mark says that Elijah must *suffer* 'as it is written of him'. No non-Christian tradition known to us speaks of the sufferings of Elijah.[2] The reference to the Son of man in *v.* 12 probably stems from mistranslation. If the tradition originally spoke of '*that* son of man', i.e. man, prophet (in Ezekiel's sense), then 9: 11–13 originally referred *only* to Elijah:

Elijah does come first to restore all things; and how is it written of that son of man [Elijah], that he should suffer many things and be treated with contempt? But I tell you that Elijah has come, and they did to him whatever they pleased, as it is written of him.[3]

[1] J. Jeremias, ''Ηλ(ε)ίας', *TWNT*, II, 930–43, traces the genealogy of the idea from Mal. 4: 5 f. to Sirach 48: 1–12 *a*; Eth. Enoch 89: 52; 90: 31; 93: 8; I Macc. 2: 58; Philo, *Deus Imm.* 136–9; Jos. *Ant.* 8, 324; 4 Ezra 6: 26; 7: 109; S. Bar. 77: 24; Sib. II, 187–9; Martyrdom Isa. 2: 14–16; Justin, *Dial.* 8: 4; 49: 1; Pirke R. Eli'ezer 43; bPes. 70b Bar.; jPes. 3, 30b, 25; and the late-Jewish Elijah-apocalypses.

[2] In Mark 9: 11 the disciples cite the Elijah belief as an objection to Jesus' prediction of his suffering and death, for the restoration of all things which Elijah is to effect three days before the end makes messianic suffering superfluous (Jeremias, ''Ηλ(ε)ίας', p. 939). It appears obvious then that the idea of Elijah's sufferings is alien to the Jewish Elijah-belief. Matthew confirms this conclusion when he omits both appeals to Scripture in his account (17: 9–13) and introduces the identification of John with Elijah in 11: 14 as an idea which his hearers are unprepared to receive (εἰ θέλετε δέξασθαι).

In Rev. 11: 3–12 the 'two witnesses' (Moses and Elijah) appear before the end to effect repentance, but undergo martyrdom at the hands of the beast. The Jewish substrata are clear, but the idea of martyrdom here is a Christian innovation growing out of both the crucifixion of Jesus and the persecution under Domitian.

The Coptic Elijah apocalypse, which Jeremias (*op. cit.* pp. 942 f.) cites as evidence for a pre-Christian view of a suffering Elijah, is obviously a haggadic expansion of Rev. 11: 3–12.

Elijah did suffer (I Kings 19: 2, 10); but there is no basis for the much-advanced conjecture that pre-Christian apocalyptists expected Elijah to suffer at his return (as, e.g., Dibelius, *Johannes der Täufer*, p. 30 n. 2, and Jeremias, *op. cit.*).

[3] Professor Cyril C. Richardson suggested this reconstruction to me. Bultmann, *The History of the Synoptic Tradition*, p. 125, considers *v.* 12 *b* to be a post-Markan interpolation from Matt. 17: 12; so also Lohmeyer, *Das Evangelium des Markus* (1951), p. 183 n. 1. H. E. Tödt decisively refutes this conjecture, but fails to account adequately for the undeniably abrupt shift from John to Jesus in *v.* 12 *b* (*The Son of Man in the Synoptic Tradition*, tr. by D. M. Barton, 1965, pp. 169, 196).

If this was the original meaning, then obviously the passage has a pre-Markan history and Mark cannot be said to have created the identification of Elijah with John. Nevertheless he does something by this very confusion which has profound results. He links the sufferings of Elijah with those of the Son of man. Mark sets this passage after the transfiguration, the connecting link being the reference to Elijah common to each. But observe the manner in which Mark refers to Moses and Elijah on the mount: 'Elijah with Moses' (9:4). Mark's reversal of the usual order is surely secondary, since the transfiguration scene has developed as a new 'Sinai' theophany, with Moses in the more prominent place. Mark must have had strong reasons for the change (the original order still survives in 9:5). M. J. Moreton points out that Moses and Elijah do not represent the Law and the prophets, respectively; rather Moses is the representative of the old covenant, both Law and prophets, and Elijah is the eschatological restorer of all things (1:2 f.; 9:11). The stress on Elijah's presence at the transfiguration shows that the fulfilment of 'all things' (9:12) is no longer merely imminent but has arrived. The transfiguration is, as it were, the vestibule of the passion, and Elijah is present to testify to the final importance of impending events. And with him is Moses, the representative of the old covenant and the promises, now shortly to be fulfilled in the death of Jesus.[1]

Since it is immediately after the transfiguration scene that Jesus identifies Elijah with John, Mark probably intends to indicate that Jesus discovered this 'mystery' (for only he knows it) on the mount. This is part of the revelation he received as 'they were talking to Jesus' (9:4b). The secret of Jesus' messiahship (8:28–9:10) thus issues directly in the secret of John's Elijahship. The confused reference to the Son of man in v. 12, in spite of its inappropriateness, actually makes this relationship all the more clear.

Thus the identification of John with Elijah was both an act of typological-prophetic confidence and at the same time a bold, utterly amazing affirmation which turns the tables on the Jewish expectations as radically as does the reinterpretation of messiahship involving Jesus. What is expressed is the quite offensive paradox that the heavenly Elijah should be this captive, murdered prophet: a *dead* Elijah. This identification cannot be said to be a simple apologetical retort to the Jewish protest that Elijah

---

[1] In R. H. Lightfoot, *The Gospel Message of St Mark* (rev. ed., 1962), p. 117.

must first come, for this 'answer' is just as offensive as the statement that the crucified Jesus is messiah, and it operates on the same assumptions. In Mark's hands the Elijah expectation is radicalized and transformed even while the old framework is preserved.

Why then does Mark veil the account? Why does he not make the identification with John explicit? Because he has integrated the passage into his concept of the 'messianic secret'. Indeed, we might argue that part of the confusion in 9: 9–13 results from Mark's attempt to make a clear statement a mystery! This explains the restraint Mark exercises elsewhere in dealing with John's identity. Even in 1: 1–8 the 'Elijianic secret' is preserved, for Mal. 3: 1, not 4: 5 f., is quoted, and his resemblance to Elijah is only stated without comment for him who has ears to hear. If the disciples cannot comprehend Jesus' teaching about his own suffering (8: 32 f.; 9: 6, 10, 11, 32, 34), then we may fairly infer that they would not be able to understand the saying about Elijah either. They cannot because they *must* not; John's identity, like that of Jesus, is hidden until the resurrection (9: 9*b*).

This 'Elijah-theology' thus deals not just with John's relation to the Christian dispensation or the role he plays in God's redemptive activity, but is actually an expression of the core of the Christian experience of salvation. John's suffering is of a piece with Mark's views on denying oneself and taking up the cross (8: 34). John's vindication comes, not in spite of his death, but through his death and the violation of every human right and hope. His suffering is not redemptive, but it is redeemed. In Mark's eyes the suffering of John is as necessary and inevitable as the suffering of Christ, for John is the Elijah sent by God, and his suffering can only be explained by reference to God's saving purpose which triumphs in defeat. The human expectations of Elijah, colored as they are with human sin and weakness, are themselves transformed in terms of the greater wisdom of God revealed in the cross of Christ, a wisdom which is foolishness to men and certainly of no comfort to the scribes.

But John is only Elijah-incognito. The 'Elijianic secret' is but a corollary of the secret of Jesus' messiahship. Mark is not merely explaining how the Jews could have failed to recognize the messiah; he is making a statement about the essence of Christian existence. Jesus' earthly humility represents the pledge or guarantee of his triumph in glory which will subsequently be revealed.[1] A divine principle of retribution ultimately effects a reversal in human affairs: the servant *shall be* lord, the last *shall be* first. Just as the prophets (12: 2–8), so John and Jesus suffered, and so also the disciples and the church must pass through suffering and persecution before they will be vindicated. Glory always comes only *after* humiliation.[2] This creates a rift in the soteriological process which can only be bridged by faith. For suffering and glory belong to different periods, and only at the *parousia* will the ambiguity of Christian existence be ended. This unresolved bi-polarity gives to Mark's eschatology its special character.[3]

In Mark's view, then, the earthly ministry of the messiah cannot be unqualifiedly the locus of revelation. It must be revelation consonant with the character of the present period: *secret* revelation.[4] It is already clear that Mark's polarity is breaking down under the necessity to invest Jesus with *some* messianic characteristics during his life. The messianic secret is thus a compromise between humility and glorification, not a synthesis between the two.

D. CONCLUSION

Now when Mark speaks of the sufferings of John we see how completely Mark has integrated him into the gospel of Jesus Christ. John's suffering as Elijah-incognito prepares the way for the fate of Jesus, and serves as an example to the persecuted Christians in Rome. He too, like Jesus and the church, struggles in obscurity and humiliation. His true identity is concealed from the world. He too suffers an ignominious death. But he suffers as Elijah, and in that suffering shares the fate of the elect (Mark 13: 9–13). His suffering is not meaningless, any more than that which the church experiences. What 'they' (Herod and Herodias, 9: 13 referring back to 6: 17 ff.) did to him, 'they' (contemporary opponents of the church, 13: 9) will do to Christians now. *This is as it must be,* but this epoch of suffering and hiddenness will soon give way to the time of vindication, when humiliation will be swallowed up in victory.

---

[1] T. A. Burkill, 'St Mark's Philosophy of History', *NTS*, III, 2 (1956–7), 142–8; now in *Mysterious Revelation* (1963).

[2] 'Perhaps the nearest that Mark comes to a universal in his interpretation of history is that persecution is an indispensable part of the godly life' (James M. Robinson, *The Problem of History in Mark*, p. 58).

[3] Burkill, *art. cit.*   [4] *Ibid.*

CHAPTER II

JOHN THE BAPTIST IN Q[1]

A. JESUS' ESTEEM OF JOHN

To what extent do the so-called 'Q' traditions upon which Matthew and Luke drew already reflect a developed interpretation of the role of John in redemptive history? Apparently Q contained a collection of sayings concerned with the relationship between Jesus and the Baptist (Matt. 11: 2–11, 16–19; Luke 7: 18–19, 22–8, 31–5), as well as a block on the teaching of John (Matt. 3: 7–10, 11–12; Luke 3: 7–9, 16–17). If we consider other materials from the double tradition such as Matt. 11: 12–13/Luke 16: 16 and Matt. 21: 32/Luke 7: 29 f., a consistent theological perspective emerges. Many of these traditions are of high value as *ipsissima verba* of Jesus. But their cumulative effect is to throw into sharp relief John's significance for the eschatological crisis created by the presence of Jesus.

In the first place, the Q collection presents sayings which help to *create* this crisis by laying upon men the absolute demand of God in the last hour. And it is in John's preaching in Q that this demand is first heard: 'flee from the wrath to come...bear

---

[1] 'Q' technically designates that material common to Matthew and Luke which, because of similar order and vocabulary, appears to derive from an actual oral or written source which had a fixed sequence and purpose. For the sake of thoroughness, however, we will include in our discussion all the relevant material in the 'double tradition' even if its relation to Q is uncertain. Although the Q material is chronologically prior to Mark, it is placed before the chapters on Matthew and Luke due to their common dependence upon it.

The validity of analyzing Q as a literary unit is not self-evident. Even if its order and content could be agreed upon, there would still be the question of the legitimacy of a *redaktionsgeschichtliche* approach, since Q is not so much a 'redaction' as a collection, a miscellany of logia without sufficiently clear or extensive editorial data (in most cases) to allow us to speak of its viewpoint with any degree of thoroughness. Nevertheless it is necessary that the Q material be treated, not only as a prolegomenon to the study of John's role in Matthew and Luke, but also as a source for Jesus' own view of John, which serves in turn as a control for assessing the church's subsequent modifications of the John-traditions.

fruit...do not presume...the chaff he will burn with unquenchable fire' (Matt. 3: 7–12 par.).[1] The urgency of this crisis is so
extreme that even John is judged by it (Matt. 11: 2–6 par.) and
found wanting (11: 11 par.). Nevertheless, John's proclamation
participates in the activity of God; from the perspective of Q,
John is doing precisely what God desires, so much so that
rejection of John's mission is tantamount to rejection of Jesus
and the very purpose of God himself (Matt. 21: 32/Luke 7:
29 f.)!

In the second place, Q preserves sayings which illustrate
John's role in this crisis. He is more than a prophet: he is the
messenger of God who announces the imminent arrival of the
Coming One (Matt. 3: 11–12 par.; 11: 9–10 par.).[2] Even
though John's manner of serving God was in so many ways
opposite that of Jesus, John was as completely within God's will;
each fulfilled his own role in God's redemptive purpose (Matt.
11: 16–19 par.). Thus we see already in the double tradition an
eschatological schematism in which John *initiates* the messianic
crisis as the preacher of judgement and repentance (Matt. 11:
12 par.). There is no 'preparatory period', no 'between time';
John's preaching of repentance is already a part of the kingdom
of God and reveals its new quality of universal breadth, in that
it is addressed to 'the tax collectors and the harlots' (Matt. 21:

---

[1] Bultmann (*The History of the Synoptic Tradition*, p. 117) believes that
Matt. 3: 7–10/Luke 3: 7–9 and Luke 3: 10–14 are words of Jesus transferred
to John out of a desire to have some record of John's preaching of repentance.
(But cf. *Supplement*, p. 405, to p. 145.) The church is not likely to have suggested, however, that simple repentance would suffice for salvation apart
from belief in Jesus as the Christ (Percy, *Die Botschaft Jesu*, 1953, p. 9. Cf.
also Kraeling, *John the Baptist*, p. 197 n. 4, and Lohmeyer, *Johannes der Täufer*,
p. 18 n. 2).

[2] T. W. Manson, following J. Weiss and A. Merx, believes that Luke 7: 27
is an interpolation into the text of Luke due to the influence of the Gospel of
Matthew (*The Sayings of Jesus*, 1949, p. 69). The evidence for this view is
exceedingly slim. Conzelmann, *The Theology of St Luke* (1960), pp. 158 n. 5
and 167 n. 1, thinks that Luke 7: 27 is a variant of Q; so also apparently
Bultmann, *The History of the Synoptic Tradition*, p. 165. If this is so, then Q
may witness to the belief that Jesus held John to be 'the fulfilment of
Malachi's prediction of a Prophet-Messiah, and that he [Jesus] was now
looking momentarily for the kingdom of God and the Son of Man, of whose
coming John had been the divinely appointed herald and precursor' (John
Knox, 'The "Prophet" in the New Testament Christology', *Lux in Lumine:
Essays to Honor W. Norman Pittenger*, ed. by R. A. Norris, Jr., 1966, p. 26).

32).[1] It is with John, according to Q, that the decisive radicalism of the kingdom preaching begins, since he throws the kingdom open to the spiritually disinherited.[2]

The alarm caused by John's ministry to the 'lawless' and 'the poor' is reflected in Matt. 11: 12 f./Luke 16: 16.

Matt. 11: 12 f. 'From the days of John the Baptist until now the kingdom of heaven has suffered violence, and men of violence take it by force. For all the prophets and the law prophesied until John.'	Luke 16: 16. 'The law and the prophets were until John; since then the good news of the kingdom of God is preached, and every one enters it violently.'

Matthew's form of the saying stands in the context of a group of sayings about John the Baptist, Luke's in a discussion about the Law. Neither context appears to be original. Matthew's form of the saying is the more difficult and is probably older. The history of the saying shows that we are dealing with a very primitive tradition, already unintelligible by the time of the Evangelists. The parallelism of βιάζεται and ἁρπάζουσιν in Matt. 11: 12 surely denotes an act of violence in a negative

[1] F. Mussner, 'Der nicht erkannte Kairos (Matt. 11: 16–19 = Luke 7: 31–5)', *Biblica*, XL (1959), 609 n. 1.

[2] Lohmeyer, *Johannes der Täufer*, pp. 53–6, was the first to recognize the radicalism implicit in John's ministry to 'the poor'. Among his converts were tax collectors (Luke 3: 12; 7: 29; Matt. 21: 32), harlots (Matt. 21: 32) and soldiers (Luke 3: 14). These passages reveal the same tendency reflected in the frequently recurring hyperbole that '*all*' the people went out to hear him (Mark 1: 5; 11: 32 par.; Matt. 3: 5; Luke 3: 3; 7: 29; Acts 13: 24). Even Josephus reflects this tradition: 'everybody turned to John' (*Antiq.* XVIII, 5, 2). Apparently through the rite of baptism John had found a means by which the common folk and other 'sinners', who because of laxness in regard to the demands of the Law were regarded as ritually and morally 'unclean', could be regenerated apart from meticulous observance of the Law. John therefore must be credited with initiating the ministry to 'the poor', an act which the Evangelists regard as an eschatological sign in relation to Jesus (Luke 4: 18 = Isa. 61: 1 f.; Luke 14: 13, 20; Luke 7: 22/Matt. 11: 5). John's challenge to the multitudes that they should share with the wretched who have nothing (Luke 3: 11) also reflects this concern for the poor. He even describes the Coming One as a peasant or a man of the soil (chopping trees, harvesting crops) rather than as a king. Thus already in his ministry John had effected that split between the people and their leaders which was later to characterize the ministry of Jesus (*ibid.*).

sense. Kümmel therefore suggests the translation: since the appearance of the Baptist until the present moment the Kingdom of God is being violently assaulted and violent men wish to rob it.[1] This would appear to be the proper reading. But what does it mean?

F. W. Danker[2] understands the passage as an 'opposition logion'; that is, a complaint of the Pharisees against the events initiated by John, which Jesus then inverts as a testimonial to John's success. The Pharisees are muttering indignantly: 'The reign of Law and order has come to an end. This has been going on ever since John came. The kingdom of God has been publicly proclaimed and popularized, with the result that not only the righteous, but *everyone*, including publicans and sinners, forces his way in.' This is the Pharisees' basic objection. Jesus takes it up: 'And so it is true (as some of you have heard the objection voiced) that ever since John the Baptist the kingdom of heaven experiences violence, and violent men (these publicans and sinners) seize it.'

On any interpretation, however, what is remarkable about this saying from the point of view of our study is what it tells us about John the Baptist. The setting is one of conflict between Jesus and the Pharisees, but the source of the conflict is not Jesus but John. It is the old question of John's authority (cf. Mark 11: 28–33 par.). Luke's version reveals his understanding of 'the law and the prophets' as belonging to a distinct phase in redemptive history.[3] Matthew maintains his characteristic emphasis on the Scriptures as prophetic: 'all the prophets and the law *prophesied* until John.' Behind both versions lies the notion that John has somehow been the instrument of God in inaugurating the kingdom of God, and this by virtue of his indiscriminate offer of baptism to all who would repent, even tax collectors and harlots. It is unlikely that the church, engaged as it was in asserting Jesus' superiority over John, would have created a passage which credits John with the decisive act in the shift of the aeons, or that it would portray Jesus as merely John's

---

[1] *Promise and Fulfilment*, tr. by D. M. Barton (1957), p. 123; cf. E. Käsemann, *Essays on New Testament Themes*, tr. by W. J. Montague (1964), pp. 42 f.; G. Schrenck, 'βιάζομαι', *TWNT*, I, 611.

[2] 'Luke 16, 16—An Opposition Logion', *JBL*, LXXVII (1958), 231–43.

[3] Hans Conzelmann, *The Theology of St Luke* (1960), pp. 157 ff.

successor. Apparently we are to trace this eschatological conception of John's role in the preaching of the kingdom back to Jesus and, unwittingly, by way of their mumblings and grumblings, to the Pharisees themselves!

Our interpretation of Matt. 11: 12 f./Luke 16: 16 finds confirmation in the Q material of Matt. 11: 16–19/Luke 7: 31–5.

For John came neither eating nor drinking, and they say, 'He has a demon'; the Son of man came eating and drinking, and they say, 'Behold, a glutton and a drunkard, a friend of tax collectors and sinners!' (Matt. 11: 18–19.)

'This generation' is pictured as spiteful children who regard John the Baptist as an ascetic fanatic and Jesus as a profligate. Jesus does not correct their judgement but merely states it. Yet he implies a judgement on them for having seen and yet not perceived. What have they not perceived? That John's repentance preaching is the last warning signal of God before the judgement, and that the 'licentiousness' and 'lawlessness' of Jesus is the sign that the messianic kingdom has already broken in![1] The sense of the parable and its application lie in the assertion that with John and Jesus, each in his own way, the kingdom of God has suddenly become a reality among men. The poor and the sinners recognized this and thus proved to be 'children of wisdom' (Luke 7: 35); the Pharisees and scribes refused John and rejected Jesus and so showed themselves to be blind to the eschatological signs placarded before their eyes.[2] The fact that

[1] F. Mussner, 'Der nicht erkannte Kairos', *Biblica*, XL (1959), 599–602. The unity of Matt. 11: 16–19 has been challenged by Bultmann, *The History of the Synoptic Tradition*, pp. 172, 199, who regards *vv.* 16–17 as an authentic parable of Jesus to which *vv.* 18–19 have been appended as an interpretation by the Hellenistic church. Bultmann holds that the original application of the parable is irrecoverable, but it did not include reference to John.

It is probably true that the church has modified the form of the passage over time (ἦλθεν and ὁ υἱὸς τοῦ ἀνθρώπου have the appearance of technical terms); on the other hand, note the present tenses of λέγουσιν and ἔχει. Whatever the history of transmission, however, it is difficult to conceive of the church dubbing Jesus 'a glutton and a drunkard' and thus arming its opponents, or creating a parallelism of equality between John and Jesus when everywhere else it is intent on subordinating John.

[2] Cullmann, *Peter*, pp. 21 f., reminds us by a comparison of Matt. 16: 17 with John 1: 42 and 21: 15 f. that 'Jonah' can serve as a shortened form of 'Johanan' (John). It is possible then that 'the sign of Jonah' (Luke 11: 29–

Jesus conceives of his work in unity with John's in spite of their differences indicates that he has in mind a very definite role for John. He is 'more than a prophet': he is the herald of the kingdom of God (Matt. 11 : 9).[1] Even John's negativism participates in the good news, for with John the doors of the kingdom are thrown wide open to all who will submit to the judgement of God and enter.

B. LIMITATIONS PLACED ON THE ESTEEM OF JOHN

Side by side with these lofty assessments of John are two passages in Q which place a limitation on the esteem to be accorded him. The authenticity of both passages has been challenged. The first is Matt. 11 : 2–6/Luke 7 : 18–23, the story of the delegation from John the Baptist to Jesus. Kraeling argues[2] that on the face of it the question posed by John is an impossibility, for the transcendent Coming One whom he expected to destroy the wicked in unquenchable fire would scarcely be evoked by the figure of Jesus. Kraeling therefore seeks a setting in the life of the church which would account for the development of the narrative. This he finds in an early period of fraternization between Christians and the disciples of John, when lines of communication were still open and the groups regarded themselves as engaged in common cause. These Christians, most of them former disciples of John, sought to justify their faith in Jesus as the messiah, both to themselves and to those who continued to hold to the teaching of John, by appeal to Jesus' mighty works as the fulfilment of the Scriptural promises concerning the One who was to come (Isa.

30/Matt. 12: 38–41) is a deliberately veiled allusion to the repentance-preaching of John (cf. Kraeling, *John the Baptist*, pp. 136 f., who considers the Lukan form an authentic saying of Jesus). By this word-play, John is certified as a prophet in the tradition of Jonah, whose mission is the preaching of repentance prior to an act of God anticipated as judgement but received as grace. This passage would thus be one more witness to the enormous solidarity between John and Jesus, who here stakes the issue of his entire ministry on this single eschatological sign: John's preaching of repentance.

[1] Adolf Schlatter, *Das Evangelium nach Matthäus*, p. 175: 'John did not only prophesy; he was himself prophesied. He gave the people not simply hope for the future; with him began the fulfilment of this hope.'

[2] *John the Baptist*, pp. 128–31. Cf. also Bultmann, *The History of the Synoptic Tradition*, pp. 23 f.; M. Goguel, *Jean-Baptiste*, pp. 63–5; and E. Lohmeyer, *Johannes der Täufer*, p. 18.

35: 5; 61: 1).[1] The absence of a further response by John merely indicates what parties on both sides knew to be fact, that John did *not* accept Jesus as the Coming One. But the open-endedness of the narrative suggests the church's conviction, later made explicit in the Fourth Gospel, that had John lived long enough to see and hear what Christians had seen and heard, he would surely have recognized in Jesus' mighty works the tell-tale signs of the messianic Day.[2] If, however, the story of John's delegation to Jesus were essentially historical,[3] its modification for apologetic use with the Baptist community would still have proceeded along the same lines as those suggested above.[4]

In either case, then, the Q traditions reveal a situation in which the church is laboring to define John's relationship to the kingdom of heaven. Apparently Jesus' adulation of John in the verses that follow (Matt. 11: 7–9 [Q]) has become a source of embarrassment to the church. Matt. 11: 2–6 applies the antidote. The judgement implicit in *v.* 6 is that John took 'offense' at Jesus. John is therefore excluded from the kingdom of heaven, in spite of Jesus' high regard for him, since he never attained faith in Jesus as the messiah.

The necessity to clarify John's relationship to the kingdom of heaven also led to the modification of Matt. 11: 11 (= Luke 7: 28). Apparently the original logion survives only in 11: 11*a*— 'Truly, I say to you, among those born of women there has risen no one greater than John the Baptist'; to which the church

---

[1] Kraeling, *John the Baptist*, pp. 172 ff. and 130.

[2] Bultmann, *The History of the Synoptic Tradition*, p. 24, raises the faint possibility that the disciples of John had claimed for their master the fulfilment of Isa. 35: 5 f.: 'That stories of John's miracles were in circulation is in itself quite credible; for the assertion that he performed none (John 10: 41) is obviously a piece of polemic. And does not Mark 6: 14 imply that reports of the Baptist's miracles were current?' Fridrichsen, *Le Problème du Miracle* (1925), pp. 66–9, is probably closer to the truth when he says that the tension reflected here between church and Baptists arises, not because John is being declared messiah or wonderworker by his disciples, but because John's disciples believe the messiah will be altogether different from Jesus.

[3] As Dibelius argues, *Johannes der Täufer*, p. 18; so also W. G. Kümmel, *Promise and Fulfilment*, pp. 109 ff. ('. . . the Baptist appears here in no way as a witness to Christ, but as an uncertain questioner, which contradicts the tendency of the early Church to make him such a witness. . .').

[4] Examples of this modification are Matthew's use of 'the Christ' in 11: 2, or Luke's pairing of John's disciples and the addition of 7: 21.

has added the qualification in 11: 11 b—'yet he who is least in the kingdom of heaven is greater than he'. If 11: 11 a had been allowed to stand unqualified, the church's claim that Jesus was the Christ would obviously be invalidated. Therefore the church adjusted Jesus' eschatological perspective and excluded John from the time of the kingdom's realization. John may be greater than anyone in 'this generation' or any other, since through his work the eschatological crisis of judgement and salvation was faced. Nevertheless, even the least of Jesus' disciples is greater than John, because they already participate in that messianic time for which he could only hope.[1]

Here again the historical fact that John was killed before he had opportunity to enter fully into the events of Jesus' ministry is rendered as a theological judgement over him. Unwilling to suppress Jesus' high regard for John, a regard which Jesus had already in his ministry defined eschatologically, the church simply hedged Jesus' enthusiasm with qualifications which made clear their perception of the fundamental distinction between still awaiting a Coming One and accepting Jesus as the Messiah. The apologetical/polemical implications of the passage are obvious.

In short, we see the church engaged in evangelistic maneuvering with that remnant of John's disciples not already absorbed by the church. The striking fact, however, is not that the church has created or modified materials for its use, but that it has allowed Jesus' sayings about John to survive at all, embarrassing as they were to the church in its apologetical situation.

In summary, then, we find in Q and related sayings a double-sided view of John. On the one hand we see Jesus' conception

---

[1] Cullmann, 'ὁ ὀπίσω μου ἐρχόμενος', in *The Early Church* (1956), p. 180, takes up the suggestion of Franz Dibelius that 'the least' in Matt. 11: 11 b originally referred to Jesus and not to Christians generally, ὁ μικρότερος deriving from the Aramaic which means 'young' as well as 'less'. The Greek superlative here arises from a misunderstanding; the comparative is called for in parallelism with μείζων in 11: 11 a. The point is that the 'younger' (a rabbinic term for a disciple) and therefore 'lesser' of the two has become greater than his master: 'He who is least (i.e. Jesus as a disciple of John) is greater than he (i.e. John) in the kingdom of heaven.' (Cf. also Cullmann's *The Christology of the New Testament*, pp. 24, 32.) Matt. 11: 11 would thus be equivalent to Matt. 3: 11 par.

Whatever the original sense of the passage, however, its meaning in Q is obvious.

that John was the eschatological sign that the kingdom of heaven was at hand; and on the other we see the church, in extreme discomfort, seeking to circumscribe John's role and the esteem due him. The church's attempts to subordinate John only serve to heighten the impression that John was the agent through whom Jesus perceived the approach of the kingdom of heaven. Even at the fountainhead of the tradition, John is evaluated wholly in terms of his relationship to the Gospel and the kingdom of God.

CHAPTER III

JOHN THE BAPTIST IN THE GOSPEL
OF MATTHEW

We are fortunate to have in Wolfgang Trilling's analysis of 'Die Täufertradition bei Matthäus'[1] a definitive study of Matthew's treatment of John. We shall therefore make the structure of his analysis our own and supplement on the basis of it.

A. THE FATE OF A PROPHET (Matt. 14: 3–12)

Matthew abbreviates Mark's rambling account of the death of John to only a fragmentary sketch. Yet he adds two new motifs: the hostility of Herod, and the report to Jesus of John's death. Why does Matthew tell us that the disciples of John 'went and told Jesus' (Matt. 14: 12 b)? J. Schmid suggests that Matthew is establishing a causal relationship where there was none in Mark between the death of John and Jesus' subsequent withdrawal into solitude: 'Jesus flees from Herod as before the murderer of the Baptist.'[2] Matthew thereby establishes a parallel between the fate of John and the now-to-be-expected fate of Jesus; the disciples of John announce their master's death in order to proclaim to Jesus his own fate, the fate of a prophet.[3] Trilling sees three motifs emerging from this passage:

(1) The fate of the prophets. Matthew's version of the death of John is comparable to the woe pronounced over the Pharisees for building the tombs of the prophets (23: 29–36) and the parable of the vinedresser (21: 33–43). The suffering of the prophets described in these passages is actually demonstrated by the death of John; his execution is proof of the axiom that the prophet must suffer.[4] Matthew places this narrative immediately

---

[1] *BZ*, III, 2 (1959), 271–89.

[2] *Matthäus und Lukas*, p. 177, cited by Trilling, *art. cit.* p. 273.

[3] Trilling, *art. cit.* pp. 272–4.

[4] *Ibid.* p. 274. Cf. also H. J. Schoeps, *Aus frühchristlicher Zeit* (1950), pp. 126 ff. ('Die jüdischen Prophetenmorde'). The prophet's death is fateful,

after the statement that 'a prophet is not without honor except in his own country and in his own house' (Matt. 13: 57). John is the 'typical' prophet to disobedient Israel, and in typical fashion disobedient Israel slays him.[1] For this reason Matthew cannot dispense with the full report of John's beheading (as Luke does in 9: 9; 3: 19 f.), even though the account bears all the marks of bazaar-gossip.

(2) 'The anti-God front' ('Die gottfeindliche Front'). There is no mistaking the correspondence between the death of John and the Passion of Jesus: Matt. 14: 3–12 is, in fact, John's Passion. Herod himself, not Herodias, would kill John; he hesitates, not because he fears the prophet, but because he fears the people, just as in 26: 4 the high priests seek Jesus' life but fear the mob (cf. also 21: 26, 46). Herod Antipas is placed in a line with his father, who sought Jesus' life at birth (2: 13), and with his brother Archelaus, whose lordship of Judea forced Joseph to settle in Galilee (2: 22). All form a single rank of opposition. For this reason Matthew thinks it impossible that Antipas regarded John as 'a righteous and holy man' (Mark 6: 20), just as he thought it impossible that the scribe 'answered with understanding' (Mark 12: 34). In Matthew's eyes there are only two positions, and Herod stands with the murderers of the prophets.[2]

(3) This united front of opposition throws John and Jesus together. The disciples of John are Jesus' allies, Jesus' fate is tied up with John's, their enemies are the same. This parallelism of destinies already indicates a parallel purpose served by both in God's redemptive purpose.

B. THE VOCATION OF THE BAPTIST IN REDEMPTIVE HISTORY

Every statement about John the Baptist in the Gospel of Matthew is related to his function in redemptive history. Matthew develops John's role in terms of his relation to the kingdom of heaven and his identity as Elijah.

not redemptive or vicarious (Cullmann, *The Christology of the New Testament*, p. 56). It accomplishes nothing except the condemnation of the prophet-murderers.

[1] Trilling, *art. cit.* p. 274.   [2] *Ibid.* pp. 274 f.

(1) *John the Baptist and the Kingdom of Heaven*

Matt. 11: 12–13 focuses attention on this question. It seems fairly certain that 11: 12 f. is not native to the Q collection in which it stands.[1] Luke places it in an entirely different setting. Matthew has definite reasons for placing it here. In both versions of the saying the focus is not on John and the Law but rather on the two great epochs of prophecy and fulfilment: the Law and prophets on the one hand, the kingdom of heaven on the other.[2] Luke's arrangement is chronological, and commends itself as primary, yet his language shows signs of being secondary.[3] Matthew's version, on the other hand, is a grotesque jumble; 'the prophets and the law' appear in reverse order, and the sense of βιάζεται and βιασταί is anything but clear. Trilling notes that the δέ in 11: 12 obviously binds *v.* 12 to 11 (Q). But *v.* 11 contains a saying about the Baptist; therefore Matthew is apparently trying to give a more correct understanding of 11: 11 *b* by means of 12: John is (to be sure) less than 'the least in the kingdom of heaven', but from his appearance the kingdom of heaven is nevertheless here, for all the prophets prophesied until John. He is therefore obviously included in the period of the kingdom's realization.[4]

How shall we evaluate ἀπὸ δὲ τῶν ἡμερῶν...ἕως ἄρτι and ἕως Ἰωάννου? In almost every instance when Matthew uses ἀπὸ he gives it a temporal and inclusive sense, especially when used with ἕως.[5] The phrase 'the days of John' means the period of his work, ministry, activity; it is a familiar rabbinical phrase. Matthew uses it often: 24: 37 (Q)—the days of Noah; 2: 1—

---

[1] T. W. Manson, *The Sayings of Jesus*, p. 68.

[2] A third epoch is implied, when the antipathy between the world and the kingdom of heaven will be over (Kraeling, *John the Baptist*, p. 156).

[3] For example, his use of εὐαγγελίζεται to give the saying a positive significance; the fact that the kingdom is only preached, it does not arrive; and the use of the generalized πᾶς.

[4] Trilling, *art. cit.* p. 277.

[5] Trilling cites as examples Matt. 23: 35; 1: 17 (three times); 2: 16; 27: 45. Two uses of ἀπὸ appear in quotations—13: 35 and 24: 21. Cf. also Matt. 9: 22; 5: 28; 17: 18; 25: 34. Matt. 19: 4 is equal to Mark 10: 6, and Matt. 22: 46 is not certain. 'In fast allen Fällen ist ein einschliessendes Verständnis erfordert oder wenigstens nicht verhindert.' Trilling also lists examples of ἀπὸ used in the inclusive sense from the LXX and Greek literature (*ibid.* pp. 277 f. n. 38).

the days of King Herod; 23: 30—the days of our father. Thus ἀπό...'Ιωάννου means the period of John's ministry as a whole. This is made even clearer by Luke's contrasting phrase: ὁ νόμος καὶ οἱ προφῆται μέχρι 'Ιωάννου, i.e. the days of John. That Matthew intends to include John in the period of the inaugurated kingdom is already made absolutely clear in 3: 2, where he places in John's mouth the message of Jesus: 'Repent, for the kingdom of heaven is at hand.' The ἕως in 11: 13 explains how Matthew can allow John to preach the kingdom, for in his view the period of promise extends only up till the moment when John appears; with John begins the fulfilment.[1]

Matthew must also clarify the relation of the Law and the prophets to the new period in such a way as not to imply their abrogation. For this reason he adds ἐπροφήτευσαν—*not* in order to underline the prophetic role of the Baptist,[2] but on the contrary to emphasize the distinction between prophecy and fulfilment, with John serving as the inaugurator of the epoch of fulfilment.[3]

Q had said in 11: 9 that John was more than a prophet, and (if the quotation of Mal. 3: 1 originally stood in Q) intimated that this 'more' meant that he was the messenger prophesied by Malachi (Matt. 11: 10 = Luke 7: 27). Matthew makes this intimation explicit in *v.* 14. If John no longer belongs to the prophesying prophets (11: 13), if he is in reality more than a prophet, then he can no longer be understood in prophetic categories, but only in terms of categories of fulfilment. Matthew says clearly what περισσότερον προφήτου means for him: John is Elijah.

(2) *John and Elijah* (Matt. 17: 10–13; 11: 14–15)

The certainty with which the identity between John and Elijah is expressed here is unique in the New Testament. This identification comes to clearest expression in Matthew's version of the descent from the Mount of Transfiguration. Various motifs underlie Mark's parallel account (Mark 9: 11–13): the apologetical concern that if the Messiah has come so must have Elijah;

---

[1] Trilling, *art. cit.* p. 278.
[2] As Klostermann thinks, *Das Matthäusevangelium* (*Handbuch zum NT*, 4), p. 98.　　　　[3] Trilling, *art. cit.* p. 279.

the Christian belief that John is the forerunner prophesied in Mal. 3: 1 (Mark 1: 2; Matt. 11: 10; Luke 7: 27) and is therefore Elijah; and the suffering of the Baptist and the therefore prefigured fate of Jesus. Only the last, the suffering motif, has found a firm place in Mark's version.[1] The other motifs dangle like loose ends.

Matthew, however, has ordered the whole account around a single clear motif in a progression of three stages:

> *Question:* Is it true that Elijah must come?
> *Answer:* It is true.
> *Resolution:* Elijah has come; he is John!

The 'Elijianic Secret' is thereby transformed from a mystery into a dogma. John's suffering is no longer merely an intimation that Jesus will suffer ('how is it written of the Son of man, that he should suffer...?') but rather an open declaration of its inevitability and necessity ('So also the Son of man *will* suffer').

It is significant that the disciples, not Jesus, identify John with Elijah in 17: 13. Note also that 'the disciples', not the three who were with Jesus on the Mount of Transfiguration, ask about Elijah.[2] These two facts suggest that the Elijah belief is a tradition of the church placed in Jesus' mouth to gain authority. In any case, *Matthew* treats it thus.[3]

In Mark's version of the descent the crucial term is ἀποκαθ-ιστάνει—Elijah *restores* all things; in Matthew the emphasis is on ἔρχεται—Elijah *comes*. The fact of Elijah's arrival and therefore identification with John is the important thing.[4] Matthew understands this restoration in terms of Mal. 4: 5 as the ministry of repentance, and evaluates the function of John–Elijah accordingly: John preaches repentance as the condition for entry into the kingdom (Matt. 3: 2; 21: 32; 3: 11, 8).

In 11: 14 Matthew again makes explicit John's role as Elijah. But he states this bald fact in such a way that it cannot be immediately or easily grasped; it is a truth only for those who have 'ears to hear' (11: 15). It is a statement which cannot be proved

---

[1] Trilling, *art. cit.* p. 280.
[2] *Ibid.* p. 281.
[3] In 14: 1–2 Matthew deletes the parallel in Mark 6: 15 where some take Jesus to be Elijah. For him there is no longer any uncertainty: *John* is Elijah.
[4] Trilling, *art. cit.* p. 281.

but can only be apprehended by faith.[1] Thus *v.* 14 begins with the phrase καὶ εἰ θέλετε δέξασθαι—'and if you are willing to accept it, he is Elijah. . .'. But why is this difficult to receive? Because it presupposes the messiahship of Jesus, which the Jews have already (in Matthew's day) rejected.[2] The identification of John with Elijah is only a consequence of the identification of Jesus as the Messiah. It is a dogmatic expression of the relation of John to Jesus. John is not Elijah as such, but rather the Elijah of the Messiah. Here, as elsewhere in the Gospels, John's significance is defined always and only in terms of his relation to Jesus in God's plan of salvation.[3]

Whereas Mark explains the rejection of the Messiah by the 'messianic secret', Matthew attributes his rejection to the thralldom of sin (Matt. 11: 25-7). The rejection of John is explained in the same way. The children in the market-place spurn both men out of spite (11: 16-19). Herod actively desires to kill John (14: 5). The chief priests and elders opposed the purpose of God himself when they rejected John, nor did they afterward repent and believe him (21: 32). The mystery of John's identity is bound up with the mystery of Jesus'; yet it is an open mystery in that only those fail to know it who *refuse* to know it (11: 15). Even the truth about the Baptist can be known only to him to whom the Son chooses to reveal it (11: 25-7).

Thus 'he who has ears to hear' is more than a sermonic device intended to elicit reflection in the hearer;[4] it is a threat: 'You had better believe this because salvation depends on it!'[5] Matthew intensifies the menace and urgency of John's call to

[1] Trilling, *art. cit.* p. 281, quoting J. Weiss (*Schriften des NT*, I², 316) approvingly.

[2] Schweitzer, *The Quest of the Historical Jesus*, p. 383: 'From the standpoint of the eschatological expectation no one could recognize Elias in the Baptist, unless he knew of the Messiahship of Jesus.'

[3] T. W. Manson, *The Sayings of Jesus*, p. 185: 'The fact is that the identification of John with Elijah is peculiarly at home in Matthew; and it may be conjectured that the identification was made by Jewish Christians who had to meet the objection from the Jewish side that the true Messiah would be anointed and proclaimed by the returned Elijah, that this had not happened in the case of Jesus, and that therefore Jesus was not the true Messiah.'

[4] As A. H. McNeile thinks, *The Gospel According to St Matthew* (1961), p. 157.

[5] Trilling, *art. cit.* p. 281. Even if a liturgical factor is allowed for in 11: 15, its juxtaposition to 'if you are willing to accept it' in 11: 14 underlines the sense of urgency and threat.

repentance by elevating his stature in *Heilsgeschichte*. At the same time he makes belief in John's Elijianic role an article of faith. John no longer merely breaks the soil in which the seed of the Kingdom will sprout, for in Matthew John himself is the first to preach the Kingdom (3: 2). He is no longer merely a wilderness prophet, for John now speaks with the authority of the vivified Elijah himself, whose presence is a sign that prophecy has now undergone fulfilment.

C. JOHN AND JESUS

Matthew's view of the relation of John to Jesus is a consequence of his view of *Heilsgeschichte* and the fate of the prophet. John is united with Jesus but in such a manner that Jesus' superiority is maintained throughout. Trilling analyzes this relationship under the dual aspects of assimilation and distinction.

(1) *The Assimilation*

Jesus and John stand united *against* the 'anti-God front' and *for* the kingdom of heaven. The extent to which Matthew carries out this assimilation is seen in the manner in which he freely exchanges the Baptist and Jesus traditions one with another. Words of Jesus are placed in the mouth of John, and vice versa. Out of John's preaching, for example, Matthew takes the warning that 'every tree therefore that does not bear good fruit is cut down and thrown into the fire' (3: 10*b*) and places it in Jesus' parable of the fruit tree (7: 19). In 3: 10*b* it was addressed to the 'Pharisees and Sadducees', in 7: 19 it refers to Christian pseudo-prophets. In 15: 13 Matthew has Jesus apply a similar expression to the Pharisees. Again, in 12: 34 and 23: 33 Matthew places on Jesus' lips John's invective against the 'brood of vipers' (3: 7).[1] Conversely, Jesus' proclamation of the kingdom in 4: 17 is placed on the lips of John in 3: 2. The arena of conflict for John and Jesus is the same: both stand against the same array of opposition.

On the other hand, the frontal attack of Jesus against the Pharisees is carried over into the message of John. In contrast to Mark and Luke, Matthew confronts John with the Pharisees

---

[1] Trilling, *art. cit.* pp. 282 f.

from the very beginning (3: 7), with the result that the 'you' of 21 : 32 specifically indicts the Pharisees for their unbelief.[1] Recent studies have established that Matthew conceived of Judaism, not in terms of its diversity in Jesus' day, but rather in its contemporary form, that is, Pharisaical Judaism as it developed in the period following the destruction of the temple in A.D. 70.[2] Projecting backward from the present polemical situation of the church in its struggle with Pharisaic Judaism, Matthew concentrates on the Pharisees as the real opponents of Jesus, and at every opportunity makes them the villains of the piece.

Therefore the hostile front of the enemy is constituted before Jesus appears. Already the Baptist prevails against the enemies of God with acid words and the threat of judgement and wrath.[3]

John and Jesus are again placed parallel in Matt. 21 : 23–32.[4] Matthew has artfully developed the parallelism which already lay before him in Mark 11 : 27–33 by adding to it the parable of the two sons (no parallel). This parable in turn acts as a commentary on both the preceding question of authority and on the following parable of the vineyard (Matt. 21 : 33–46). Since the 'chief priests and elders' are still addressed in *vv.* 28 and 33, Matthew creates a cumulative judgement on these representatives of the anti-God front: they did not believe John (21 : 25, 32, 36). The peak of the section is *v.* 32, which serves both as the

---

[1] Matthew's reference to 'the Pharisees and Sadducees' in 3: 7 appears redactional. Cf. Matt. 16: 1–12, where four times over Matthew introduces the phrase 'the Pharisees and Sadducees' where his source had once each 'Pharisees' and 'Pharisees and...Herod' (Mark 8: 11–21). The extent to which the phrase is stereotyped in Matthew is indicated by the absence of the article before Σαδδουκαῖοι (Trilling, *art. cit.* p. 283). Reinhart Hummel comments that Matthew has no independent interest in the Sadducees, but only in connection with the Pharisees; 'Sadducees' is a collective designation for all non-Pharisaical Jews. Pairing Pharisees and Sadducees is also a slap at the Pharisees, since in rabbinical Judaism the Sadducees were considered heretics—so much as to say, 'You also are no better' (*Die Auseinandersetzung zwischen Kirche und Judentum im Matthäusevangelium*, 1963, pp. 13–22).

[2] Cf., among others, G. D. Kilpatrick, *The Origins of the Gospel According to St Matthew* (1950); Reinhart Hummel, *op. cit.*; W. D. Davies, *The Setting of the Sermon on the Mount* (1964); and W. Trilling, *Das wahre Israel. Studien zur Theologie des Matthäus-Evangeliums* (1964).

[3] Trilling, *art. cit.* p. 284.

[4] Following Trilling's analysis, *ibid.* p. 284.

application of the parable (21: 28–31) and as the reproach of the authorities for rejecting John in *v.* 25*b*. The leading idea of the whole section is therefore that these opponents have rejected the will of God. The vineyard parable which follows develops this judgement into a panorama of *Heilsgeschichte*: these opponents have always cast out God's messengers, from the prophets even to his Son. John and Jesus were rejected and suffered the fate of the prophets; John was refused belief, the Son was killed. Both are held by the people to be prophets (21: 23, 26), and for this reason their opponents in both cases 'feared' the people (21: 26, 46).[1]

In Matt. 11: 16–19 John and Jesus again stand united against the hostility of their opponents. As in 21: 32, John 'came' (ἦλθεν), and here again the word has *heilsgeschichtliche* overtones. The charge that John 'has a demon' is the same charge which is leveled against Jesus in even stronger terms in 9: 34; 12: 24; 10: 25. And 'wisdom' is served by both (11: 19*c*) just as is 'righteousness' (3: 15; 21: 32).[2]

Thus Jesus and John stand together not only in common opposition of and rejection by the opponents of God's will, but they also stand together as champions of the kingdom of heaven. Even though their methods are opposite they are both instruments of God (11: 18–19). Therefore in 4: 17 Jesus no longer says 'the time is fulfilled' (Mark 1: 15), because for Matthew the epoch of salvation has already dawned with the preaching of John. Matthew therefore redefines the central thrust of John's message: not baptism, but the kingdom of heaven (3: 2)![3]

John is therefore taken up into the epoch of the inaugurated kingdom of God. He stands not on the other side but on this side of the eschatological divide which separates the old from the new time. With his appearance the kingdom begins to arrive.[4] No other evangelist dares to assimilate John to Jesus so closely.

[1] Cf. J. Jeremias, *The Parables of Jesus* (1954), p. 64.

[2] Trilling, *art. cit.* p. 284.

[3] *Ibid.* p. 285. Trilling notes that John's message has been ordered by Matthew along the same lines as Jesus'. Both proclaim salvation before they threaten judgement. John cries 'The Kingdom!' before he threatens with the ax, just as Jesus in the Sermon on the Mount offers the Beatitudes before the words of menace.

[4] *Ibid.* p. 286.

(2) The Distinction

Matthew's view of John is two-sided, however. The distinction between Jesus and John which he finds in his sources is made even sharper. Precisely because of their extensive assimilation the need arises to maintain the necessary boundaries. Only Jesus is Messiah! The Baptist must not be allowed to jeopardize the unique place of Jesus.[1]

Therefore the power to mediate the forgiveness of sin is denied John's baptism. Only the blood of Christ brings about forgiveness (26: 28—'this is the blood of the covenant, which is poured out...for the forgiveness of sins'). John's is only a βαπτίζω... εἰς μετάνοιαν (3: 11a); Mark's reference to the forgiveness of sins is deleted. In 3: 11b Matthew re-orders the verse so that the emphasis falls on ἰσχυρότερός μου ἐστίν instead of ἐρχόμενος, so that John is made to admit frankly that Jesus is his superior.[2] Because John is subordinate to Jesus he is therefore unworthy to baptize him (3: 14). We see here not a polemical thrust at the inferiority of John's baptismal rite (as opposed to Christian) but a reflection on his person: '*I* need to be baptized by you.' Jesus is superior to John, yet Matthew does not thereby obliterate John: 'It is fitting for *us* to fulfil all righteousness' (3: 15). John's modesty is overruled; it is well that he is modest, but it is also well that he baptize the Messiah, for in so doing he fulfils the will of God ('righteousness'—3: 15b; 21: 32). The word δικαιοσύνη does not spill out by accident; it is Matthew's peculiar way of designating the faith and life of Christians and of Christianity in general (cf. 5: 6, 10; 6: 1 ff.).[3] In undergoing John's baptism, Jesus declares baptism obligatory for believers and gives at the same time a more elevated meaning to John's rite; baptism is in fact the constitutive element of Christian righteousness (28: 19)![4] The sense of πληρῶσαι may also be involved here: in the baptism of Jesus *John's baptism is fulfilled*, i.e. Christianized, and

[1] Trilling, *art. cit.* p. 286.

[2] Dibelius, *Johannes der Täufer*, p. 55.

[3] A. Fridrichsen, '"Accomplir toute justice"', *Congrès d'histoire du Christianisme: Jubilé Alfred Loisy*, ed. P.-L. Couchoud (1928), I, 167–77. Cf. also Georg Strecker, *Der Weg der Gerechtigkeit. Untersuchung zur Theologie des Matthäus* (1962).

[4] Fridrichsen, *art. cit.* p. 176.

becomes by this act the rite of the church. No comparison between inferior Baptist baptism and superior Christian baptism is intended,[1] for John's rite is stamped with the authority of God and already is marked out as the way of 'righteousness' (21: 32). The meaning of πληρῶσαι is made clear by 5: 17; Jesus comes not to destroy but to *fulfil* John's rite in such a way that its consummation is at the same time its transformation.[2] Thus Matthew also changes the voice at baptism from private to public address in order to make it the divine authorization of the Christian baptismal rite established by the Messiah.[3]

Matthew therefore makes his point: John is subordinate to Jesus. Yet Matthew subordinates him in such a way that the distinction is itself subordinated to the unity between them. Each has a share in manifesting the Christian rite of baptism to the world.

Even the fact that both Jesus and John preach the kingdom conceals a distinction between them. When John calls 'Repent, for the kingdom of heaven is at hand', Matthew attaches to it Isa. 40: 3; the rationale for repentance is that the way is now being prepared for the Lord (Matt. 3: 2 f.). But when Jesus uses the same phrase in 4: 17, Matthew introduces it by Isa. 9: 1–2, changing all the LXX futures to the perfect tense.[4] In both cases

[1] Matthew does not anticipate a Pentecost; John's prophecy of a Spirit-baptism is apparently fulfilled when Jesus is baptized. Thus 3: 11 relates to 3: 16 as prophecy to fulfilment. (Cf. G. Bornkamm, 'End-Expectation and Church in Matthew', in *Tradition and Interpretation in Matthew*, tr. by P. Scott, 1963, p. 36.)

[2] Fridrichsen, *Congrès d'histoire du Christianisme*, pp. 175 f. Cf. also Bultmann, *The History of the Synoptic Tradition*, p. 252: '...in the early Church the story of Jesus' Baptism was soon conceived of in this sense as a cult legend. Jesus was the first who received the Baptism of water and the Spirit, and by that inaugurated it as an efficacious rite for believers.'

[3] Fridrichsen, *Congrès d'histoire du Christianisme*, p. 176. Matthew has changed Mark's εἰς αὐτόν to ἐπ' αὐτόν in 3: 16. Luke's identical change appears to be coincidental and not based on a Q account of the baptism (Bultmann, *The History of the Synoptic Tradition*, p. 251). If this is so, then Matthew may regard the baptism as an anointing of the Messiah and the coming of the Spirit as his being 'crowned'. Cf. Odes of Sol. 1: 1—'the Lord is upon my head as a crown', and identical conceptions in 5: 12 and 17: 1. Justin Martyr (*Dial. Trypho* 8, 4 and 49, 1) says that Elijah is commissioned to anoint the messiah. It is difficult to determine the extent to which Justin's statement has been colored by the Gospel of Matthew, however.

[4] Bornkamm, *Jesus of Nazareth*, pp. 51 f.

prophecy is fulfilled, the Scripture is cited as a now accomplished fact; but John, we are given to understand, is the forerunner, Jesus is the 'light' which 'has dawned' (4: 16), i.e. the messiah. The assimilation of their messages does not wipe out the distinction of their roles in God's redemptive purpose.

The scribe Matthew (13: 52) has a very clear conception of discipleship patterned after the rabbinic example: the disciple follows his master.[1] It is all the more remarkable then that Matthew portrays Jesus as the *disciple of John*. There is no other way to interpret his retention of ὀπίσω μου in 3: 11. Likewise in 4: 12 and 17 Matthew shows that Jesus is John's successor. In 14: 13 Jesus withdraws not just because John is dead but because Herod regards him as the new head of John's movement (14: 2). But Matthew is willing to picture Jesus as John's disciple only because at the same time he provides safeguards. Thus in 3: 11 ὀπίσω μου is juxtaposed to ἰσχυρότερός μου ἐστίν and 4: 17 is preceded by 4: 16. Jesus is the disciple who outshines his master.[2]

The same balance between subordination and exaltation exists in 11: 12–15. Matthew preserves Q's word about John's being least in the kingdom of heaven (11: 11b/Luke 7: 28b), but he does not develop it. He centers rather on the phrase 'more than a prophet' (11: 9).[3] 11: 12–15 is concerned strictly with *Heilsgeschichte* and elevates John above any previous estimation of him in Matthew's sources. The same attitude appears in Matthew's use of 11: 2–6 (Q). If John was 'offended' by Jesus Matthew does not tell us so, nor does he pass judgement on John. Instead Matthew builds out of the Q collection a massive demand for repentance (11: 2–30), and emphasizes throughout the positive role played by John. It is as if the phrase 'blessed is he who takes no offense at me' of 11: 6 is addressed to all men and no longer to John.[4]

---

[1] Matt. 4: 19; 8: 19, 22 f.; 9: 9; 10: 24, 38; 11: 28; 16: 24; 19: 21. Cf. Bornkamm, 'End-Expectation and Church in Matthew', *op. cit.* pp. 15 ff.

[2] Matt. 11: 11b may also indicate that Jesus is a disciple of John who nevertheless surpasses him (cf. above, p. 25 n. 1).

[3] Trilling, 'Die Täufertradition bei Matthäus', *BZ*, III, 2 (1959), 287.

[4] Cf. in this connection Paul Schubert, 'The Structure and Significance of Luke 24', *Neutestamentliche Studien für Rudolf Bultmann*, p. 180, who notes that Matt. 11: 2–6 serves a structurally climactic purpose for Matthew. In his first large section Matthew has taken great care to furnish at least one specific

Thus, though Matthew is careful to distinguish John from Jesus, he does so with reserve. His real concern is to make John an ally in the kingdom of heaven. John is no threat; Matthew speaks of him with complete impartiality. Of tension between Jesus' and John's disciples, of opposition between the two camps, of polemic against John's followers as is reflected in John 1: 19 ff., there is not a trace.[1] Three passages in Matthew mention John's disciples. In 9: 14 the question of fasting is brought by 'the disciples of John'; in Mark's version 'people came' and in Luke the Pharisees asked it (Mark 2: 18; Luke 5: 33). In Matthew's account of the question there is no evidence of polemic against a *current* Baptist practice, since Christians also fast (Matt. 6: 16–18). No hostility is shown the disciples of John, even though the saying about new patches and new wine which follows in the triple tradition tends to place them in the same camp as the Pharisees (9: 16 f.). Matt. 11: 2–6 and 14: 12 also show the disciples of John going to Jesus, again without hostility. Since 14: 12 is the most clearly redactional of the three passages, it may be taken to express Matthew's attitude toward the Baptists, and here they seek Jesus out as an ally. It would be an overstatement to say, as does Trilling, that Matthew treats John's disciples as if they were Christians,[2] for they do not have the bridegroom (9: 15). Matthew rather relegates them to limbo; they are neither Christians nor opponents. Apparently Matthew does not have to define their relationship to the church because they posed no problem for the church for which he wrote.[3] The Baptist and his disciples enter the picture only as elements of the past ('John came'—11: 18; 21: 32).

and detailed illustration of every item in the synoptic list of Isaianic prophecies (11: 4b; cf. also 10: 7–8): Go and tell John what you hear and see: the blind receive their sight (9: 27–31), and the lame walk (8: 5–18; 9: 1–8); lepers are cleansed (8: 1–4), and the deaf hear (9: 32–4); and the dead are raised up (9: 18–26); and the poor (cf. 5: 3; 10: 8b–10; 11: 28) have good news preached to them (5: 1–12; 9: 35–11: 1; 11: 28–30). Such a comprehensive summary clearly diverts attention from John.

[1] Trilling, *art. cit.* p. 286. The fact that Matthew introduces little new material concerning the Baptist is another indication that the church for which he wrote was not polemically engaged with John's disciples.

[2] *Ibid.*

[3] Dibelius (*From Tradition to Gospel*, p. 259) treated Matt. 11 as a complex of materials for use in warding off Baptist opponents. But Matt. 11, quite to the contrary, has as its motif the *Jews'* rejection of both Jesus and John. The

D. CONCLUSION

Matthew has fabricated out of the diverse materials at his disposal a compact and consistent conception of the role of John. He betrays no biographical interest in John whatsoever; John remains remote as a person. Matthew's point of departure in adapting and modifying his sources is the Elijah-concept. By making John's role unmistakably clear, Matthew introduces an element of certainty which admits of no ambiguity: John is the prophesied Elijah. By this means the elevation and assimilation of John does not endanger the unique significance of Jesus for salvation. In addition, other Christological safeguards were added to make clear John-the-Elijah's subordination to Jesus-the-Messiah.

But apart from these touches the drift of Matthew's whole effort is toward the 'Christianization' of John. John stands on the other side from the 'prophets and the law', he inaugurates the messianic kingdom and belongs to the time of its realization and arrival.[1] John's baptism and preaching of repentance are no longer considered to be elements restricted to the preparation of the way, but have become essential signs of the kingdom itself and indispensable for entry into it. Like Jesus, John proclaimed the kingdom and threatened opponents with the wrath of judgement; like Jesus he was refused belief and was killed. John's fate prepared the fate of Jesus. He was a Christian martyr before Christ died. Herein lies the one polemical note in Matthew's use of John, a polemic directed not against the Baptist movement but against that portion of Israel which rejected Jesus, the 'anti-God front'. Behind the entire Gospel of Matthew lies the contention that the church alone is the *true* Israel.[2] John is a witness against both 'that' generation and 'this' that they have rejected the will of God and have lost the keys to the kingdom (21 : 43). Claim is therefore laid on John by the 'true' people of God. It is this deep gulf dividing the two

only touches of polemic against John were already in Q and are neutralized by Matthew's positive evaluation of him.

[1] Trilling, *art. cit.* p. 289. In this light 11 : 11 *b* does not *exclude* John from the kingdom in Matthew's eyes; it merely subordinates him *within* it.

[2] Cf. Trilling, *art. cit.* p. 289; and, by the same author, *Das wahre Israel* (1964).

'Israels' which accounts perhaps more than anything else for the fact that Matthew has quartered John within the Christian camp.

Matthew has made explicit everything in Mark's picture of John which lay hidden: the Herodian opposition, the fate of the prophet, his identity as Elijah. But by so doing he has completely altered the representation. In Mark, John's fate as Elijah-incognito had expressed the ambiguity and suffering of Christian existence in the interval before Christ's coming again. But now in Matthew, John's fate illustrates the hostility of 'pseudo-Israel' to every overture from God. John's identity as Elijah serves both to make his murder all the more inexcusable, and to validate the messiahship of Jesus according to the demands of the proof-from-prophecy schematism. If Matthew's treatment is thus more comprehensive than Mark's, it is also—at least from the point of view of this writer—less profound.

CHAPTER IV

JOHN THE BAPTIST IN THE GOSPEL OF LUKE

A. JOHN THE BAPTIST IN THE BODY OF LUKE'S GOSPEL (Luke 3–24)

(1) *Jesus, John and Elijah in Luke*

When we turn from Matthew's portrayal of John the Baptist to that in the Gospel of Luke, we are struck by a remarkable difference. Luke has retained nothing of John's role as Elijah. To be sure, he was probably unfamiliar with Matthew's explicit identification of John with Elijah (Matt. 17: 10–13; 11: 14). But even Mark's intimations of this identification have been suppressed by Luke.[1] Likewise, where he can, Luke omits references to resurrected prophets, notably Elijah (Mark 15: 34 f. = Matt. 27: 47—the cry of dereliction),[2] and even those which he retains he makes the opinions of Herod or the crowd and discredits.[3]

On the other hand, while Luke deletes five of Mark's nine references to Elijah, he adds three of his own—1: 17; 4: 25, 26. In each case he rejects the concept of the eschatological return of Elijah already familiar to us from Malachi, Mark and Matthew. Elijah is for Luke the epitome of the Spirit-filled prophet, mighty in word and deed. He is the true prophet, the prophet *par excellence* of the Old Testament. There is thus no Elijah typology; neither John nor Jesus *fulfil* anything as 'new Elijahs'. Luke uses Elijah purely as a basis for comparison. For

[1] Mark 9: 9–13 (Elijah has come) and 1: 6 (the 'Elijianic' description of John's garments) are absent from Luke.

[2] Hans Conzelmann, *The Theology of St Luke*, tr. by G. Buswell (1960), p. 51 n. 1 (for this and all subsequent citations the fourth edition, 1962, of *Die Mitte der Zeit* has been consulted).

[3] Luke 9: 7–9, 19–21 (Conzelmann, *op. cit.* pp. 25, 167). At the transfiguration (Luke 9: 30–3), Moses and Elijah appear as representatives of the old dispensation, but only in order to be superseded; they 'part' (διαχωρίζεσθαι) from Jesus, and when the cloud dissipates Jesus is found *alone* ('Ιησοῦς μόνος).

instance, in Luke 4: 24–7 Jesus is, like Elijah and Elisha, a prophet without honor in his own country. Likewise in Luke 1: 17, John 'will go before him in the spirit and power of Elijah, to turn the hearts of the fathers to the children'. The reference to Mal. 4: 5 f. is unmistakable, yet Luke resists identifying John as Elijah *redivivus* who will restore all things; he will only be *like* Elijah, i.e. a mighty prophet of repentance.[1] John 'will' not restore all things because he *did* not restore all things. In Luke's theology this restoration awaits the *parousia* at the end of history.[2] At that time *Jesus* will restore all things (Acts 3: 21—ἀποκατάστασις).

Luke 7: 27 must therefore be understood in the light of 1: 17. Luke is willing to quote the passage in Mal. 3: 1 which he may have found here in Q,[3] but he does not go on to say, as does Matthew, that the messenger of Malachi is 'Elijah who is to come' (Matt. 11: 14).

Thus Luke divests John of the role of Elijah *redivivus* which Mark had suggested and Matthew had developed. He has remained faithful to the concept of Q in which John is the fore-runner of the Messiah and nothing else. Yet at the same time we see Luke developing a comparison between *Jesus* and Elijah, not in order to portray Jesus as the eschatological prophet of the end-time (for Acts 3: 21 does not do this) but in order to estab-lish Jesus' authority as 'a great prophet' (7: 16). Not once is Jesus 'the' prophet; he is only 'a prophet' (4: 24; 7: 16, 39; 22: 64; 24: 19; Acts 3: 22 f.; 7: 37). Luke develops not an Elijah typology but rather *an Elijah-midrash* based on the account of Elijah in the Books of Kings. Jesus is compared with Elijah because in no other Old Testament prophet did the Spirit of God work so mightily. P. Dabeck[4] has analyzed the parallels (several of which I have added):

---

[1] Lukanisms abound in 1: 17—καὶ αὐτὸς, προέρχομαι, ἐνώπιον, the phrase ἐν πνεύματι καὶ δυνάμει (Benoit, 'L'Enfance de Jean-Baptiste selon Luc 1', *NTS*, III, 1956–7, 181), so that Luke must be held responsible for the ideas expressed. The fact that Luke uses ἐπιστρέψαι instead of ἀποκαταστήσει (Mal. 3: 23 LXX) indicates that he is not concerned to portray John as Elijah *redivivus*. Cf. also C. H. Dodd, *Historical Tradition in the Fourth Gospel* (1963), p. 265.

[2] Conzelmann, *The Theology of St Luke*, pp. 17 and 101 n. 1.

[3] Cf. above, p. 19 n. 2.

[4] 'Siehe, es erschienen Moses und Elias', *Biblica*, XXIII (1942), 175–89.

Luke 4: 25—Jesus is rejected as were Elijah and Elisha;

Luke 7: 11–17—the account of Jesus' raising of a widow's son parallels a similar act by Elijah, and each miracle evokes faith (I Kings 17: 24);

Luke 9: 54—Jesus refuses to call down fire on his opponents (II Kings 1: 9–12); but

Luke 12: 49—Jesus did come to cast fire upon the earth (I Kings 18: 20–40; II Kings 1: 9 ff.);

Luke 12: 50–3—Jesus rejects the role of Elijah in Mal. 4: 5 f.;

Luke 12: 54–6—Jesus refers to a 'cloud rising in the west' as a sign (= I Kings 18: 44);

Luke 24: 50–3—like Elijah, Jesus *ascends* to heaven (II Kings 2: 11; cf. also Acts 1: 9);

Acts 1: 11—Jesus' disciples, like Elisha, stand gazing into heaven after him (II Kings 2: 12);

Acts 1: 9—a cloud takes Jesus from sight (II Kings 2: 12; Luke 9: 34–6);

Luke 9: 61 f.—Jesus' call of a disciple is phrased in language borrowed from Elijah's call of Elisha (I Kings 19: 20 f.);

Luke 9: 51—'received up' (ἀναλήμψεως) refers to Jesus' ascension; the same word is used of Elijah's ascension (II Kings 2: 1—ἐγένετο...ἀνάγειν; 2: 9—ἀναλημφθῆναί; 2: 11—ἀνελήμφθη);

Luke 24: 49 and/or Acts 1: 4 f.—Jesus tells his disciples to 'stay' or 'wait' until they are 'clothed' with power from on high, just as Elijah charged Elisha to wait until he would be 'clothed' with Elijah's mantle (II Kings 2: 4, 6, 9);

Luke 12: 24—'consider the *ravens*' (I Kings 17: 1–7);

Luke 22: 43—a ministering angel (I Kings 19: 4–8);

Luke 3: 21; 9: 18, 28 f.; 11: 1; 22: 32, etc.—Jesus as a man of prayer; Elijah was the man of prayer *par excellence* in the Old Testament (I Kings 17: 20–2; 18: 36 f., 42; 19: 4, 9–18; II Kings 1: 10, 12; cf. James 5: 17 f.).

None of this material appears in the other Gospels in precisely this form. Enough of the parallels between Elijah and Jesus suggested above possess sufficient cogency to merit the conclusion that Luke has created or heightened the correspondences. In many cases Luke's purpose is simply to illustrate the teaching of Jesus by means of the Elijah narratives (cf. especially Luke 9: 61 f.; 12: 24). It is, of course, only because John is not

Elijah that Luke is free to develop the exegetical analogy between Elijah and Jesus.

This 'Elijah-midrash' is, however, only at best a secondary motif in Luke's Gospel. It is merely one of several minor themes originating out of the desire to assimilate all honorific and exalted titles to Jesus Christ.[1] As Conzelmann has shown, Luke is 'promiscuous' in his use of messianic titles. For him, Christ, Prophet, Son of God, King, Son of Man, Chosen One, etc., are equivalent.[2] Jesus is compared to Elijah only because Elijah is the greatest of the Old Testament prophets, and in the comparison Jesus is made even greater than he. In the process, however, the eschatological role of Elijah popularized by Mal. 4: 5 f. and Sirach 48: 10 is utterly rejected, not just because of its unfamiliarity to Gentiles,[3] but primarily because this expectation had been shattered by history itself: when John the Baptist and Jesus came, all things were *not* 'restored', the Kingdom did *not* come, the fathers were *not* turned to the sons. The rejection of the eschatological Elijah motif by Luke is but one step in his reinterpretation of eschatology and redemptive history as a whole.

---

[1] Cf., for instance, references in Luke where aspects of Jesus' ministry are described in terms reminiscent of Moses: the use of ἔξοδος to describe his passion (9: 31) and of ἐξήγαγεν to describe his ascension (24: 50); the use of Deut. 18: 15 f. where a prophet like Moses is promised (Acts 3: 22 ff.; 7: 37); the designation of seventy disciples (Luke 10: 1) equivalent to Moses' selection of seventy elders (Exod. 24: 1); emphasis on the ascension of Jesus to heaven, comparable to that of Moses in Jewish legend; and the use of the Sinaitic command 'Hear him' at the transfiguration (Luke 9: 35) (cf. Jindřich Mánek, 'The New Exodus in the Books of Luke', *Novum Testamentum*, II, 1958, 8–23).

[2] *The Theology of St Luke*, pp. 170–4. Nevertheless, the identification of Jesus as 'the Prophet' in a Christological sense is never made clear and forthright by Luke, although it seems to be implied (cf. especially Acts 7: 37 and 3: 22–6). Apparently the view that John was the eschatological prophet, shared by Baptists and Christians alike, preempted the use of the title 'Prophet' for Jesus until quite late (as in the Fourth Gospel) (cf. John Knox, 'The "Prophet" in the New Testament Christology', *Lux in Lumine*, p. 25).

[3] As Goguel thought (*Life of Jesus*, p. 276 n. 2). We may reject the conclusion of J. A. T. Robinson, 'Elijah, John and Jesus: An Essay in Detection', *NTS*, IV (1957–8), 276, who argues that 'Luke omits both the passages in which Jesus proposes his tentative identification of John with Elijah. For him the person of the Baptist is no longer a mystery: he is Elijah from birth (i. 16 f.).' If this is so (and we have seen that it is not), why then would Luke omit those passages which identify John as Elijah?

(2) The Role of John the Baptist in Luke

The work of Hans Conzelmann on the significance of John the Baptist in Luke's Gospel is so important that we shall summarize it in detail and then offer a critique. According to Conzelmann, Luke conceives of the history of redemption as divided into three epochs or stages:

(1) The period of Israel (Luke 16: 16); the epoch of the Law and the Prophets, ending with John;

(2) The period of Jesus' ministry (not of his 'life'), in three phases:

> (a) The period of the gathering of 'witnesses' in Galilee beginning from the Baptism ('Galilee'),
>
> (b) The journey of the Galileans to the Temple ('The Journey'),
>
> (c) The period of the teaching in the Temple, the Passion, Resurrection and Ascension ('Jerusalem');

(3) The period since the Ascension and before the Parousia, i.e. the period of the Church and the Spirit.

The Parousia itself does not represent a stage within the course of this saving history, but the end of it.[1] In this carefully defined schematism John the Baptist is relegated to the first stage. He is the last of the prophets, whose proclamation of repentance paves the way for the arrival of the second epoch of salvation inaugurated by Jesus at his baptism (Luke 3: 21 f.) and publicly proclaimed at the synagogue in Nazareth (Luke 4: 18 ff.). Luke therefore completely separates John from Jesus in Luke 3: 1–20; by a literary *tour de force* John is imprisoned *before* he baptizes Jesus (3: 19 f.), even though his presence is assumed in 3: 21 f.

The reference to the imprisonment in iii, 19 f. divides the section concerning John from the section concerning Jesus in the sense of drawing a distinction between the epochs of salvation, for which xvi, 16 provides the clue. Now the way is open for the story of Jesus. The fact that the activity of the two still overlaps cannot be entirely eliminated, but Luke deprives it of any real significance.[2]

---

[1] Conzelmann, *The Theology of St Luke*, pp. 16 f. Helmut Flender's important study is largely dependent on Conzelmann's analysis of the Baptist materials (*St Luke, Theologian of Redemptive History*, tr. by R. H. and Ilse Fuller, 1967, pp. 21 f., 50, 85 f., 122–8, etc.).

[2] Conzelmann, *The Theology of St Luke*, p. 21.

John therefore marks the division between two epochs in the continuous history of salvation, though he himself belongs to the earlier of the two epochs which meet at this point. Eschatological events do not break out after John, that is, the kingdom of God does not arrive; the kingdom will come only at the close of the third and final epoch (the epoch of the church), when history itself will draw to an end. Thus, unlike Mark, Luke cannot say that the kingdom is at hand as a result of John's mission (Mark 1: 14 f.), he can say only that the kingdom begins to be preached after John's work (Luke 16: 16).[1] As a result of Jesus' ministry the kingdom does not *come*, but disciples of Jesus can now 'see' it as a future inevitability and can receive strength from this vision in order to endure the interim period in which the church struggles with the world.[2]

Because the kingdom has lost its eschatological imminence and has been removed to the remote future, John's relation to it is ruptured. When Luke speaks of John preaching good news to the people (3: 18—εὐηγγελίζετο), there is no mention of the imminence of the kingdom.[3] The 'good news' is that the time of expectation characterized by the Law and the prophets has come to a close and the period of fulfilment has begun.[4] But the epoch of expectation is complemented rather than superseded by the epoch of fulfilment as 16: 16 shows: '...until now there was "only" the law and the Prophets, but from now on there is "also" the preaching of the Kingdom.'[5] Thus John's relation to the central period of salvation is one both of continuity and discontinuity: discontinuity, in that his work belongs to the period of promise and is thus relegated to a prologue (3: 1–20); continuity, in that the preaching of repentance characterized by the whole period of the Law and prophets continues on into the new period as a prerequisite for accepting Jesus.[6] Thus Luke 16: 16, which Conzelmann says *excludes* John (along with the Law and the prophets) from the period in which the kingdom is preached, is followed by 16: 17, which establishes the enduring validity of the former epoch.

[1] Conzelmann, *The Theology of St Luke*, p. 23.
[2] *Ibid.* pp. 113 ff. Key references are Luke 22: 16, 18, 30, 69; 13: 28 f.; 23: 42; Acts 14: 22.
[3] *Ibid.* p. 23 n. 1. [4] *Ibid.* p. 159 n. 1.
[5] *Ibid.* p. 23. [6] *Ibid.*

Thus John has a clearly defined function in the centre of the story of salvation. As it is his ministry rather than his person that serves as a preparation for Jesus, he is subordinate to the work of Jesus in the same way as is the whole epoch of the Law.[1]

Because the kingdom has been shifted to the remote future in Luke's conception, John can no longer be regarded as its fore-runner. He is not Elijah, he is only, like Elijah, a prophet. John is the last and greatest of the prophets, but his status does not carry him beyond the period of the prophets, for he does not pro-claim the kingdom of God. Not even at the end of history will there be a forerunner; the kingdom will come 'suddenly' so that there can be no advance proclamation by a forerunner (Acts 3: 20 f.).[2]

Conzelmann finds confirmation for his analysis of Luke's theological treatment of John in Luke's geographical motifs.[3] It has long been recognized that Luke believed 'the wilderness' region to be distinguished from 'the Jordan'. Never having been there he assumes that river valleys are fertile and that the Jordan cannot be accounted a part of the wilderness. He thus has John *leave* 'the wilderness' and go into 'all the region about the Jordan' (3: 2 f.). The Jordan thus becomes the locale of John. He is, according to Conzelmann, never anywhere else. After his baptism Luke has Jesus explicitly *return* from the Jordan and enter the wilderness (Luke 4: 1); the other Gospels do not distinguish between the two areas so sharply. Subsequently Jesus never enters John's domain. The only reference in Mark or Q which places Jesus in the Jordan region after his baptism is dropped by Luke (Mark 10: 1). Luke also consistently avoids the geographical hyperbole used in Mark 1: 5 and elsewhere ('there went out to him all the country of Judea, and all the people of Jerusalem') and replaces it instead with a generalized hyperbole ('all the people' went out—Luke 3: 21; 7: 29; 16: 16; 20: 6; Acts 13: 24). At the same time he applies the geo-graphical hyperbole to the success of *Jesus* (5: 17; 6: 17; 7: 17)! Conzelmann contends that these shifts are deliberate, for Luke wants to associate John only with the Jordan and reserve Judea

---

[1] Conzelmann, *The Theology of St Luke*, p. 24.

[2] *Ibid.* p. 101. Conzelmann notes that in Acts 3: 20 f. Luke applies the Elijah 'typology' to Christ (p. 101 n. 1), but he fails to notice elsewhere the extent to which Jesus is compared to Elijah (see above, pp. 43 f.).

[3] *Ibid.* pp. 18–22.

and Galilee as the specific domain of Jesus. Jesus does go to Jericho (18: 35; 19: 1), but Luke probably did not know its real location. Conzelmann concludes, therefore, that 'the Jordan is the region of the Baptist, *the region of the old era*, whereas the ministry of Jesus lies elsewhere. In any case "Judaea", when connected with John, is consistently omitted in contrast with the parallel passages.'[1]

Conzelmann's treatment of John has received so much attention that a detailed critique of his position seems necessary.

Geographical motifs in Luke's presentation of John

There is some truth in Conzelmann's assertion that John is associated with the Jordan.[2] Yet, on the other hand, Luke omits all of Mark's references to the Jordan (Mark 1: 5, 9; 3: 8; 10: 1) and has but one reference in common with Matthew (Matt. 3: 5 = Luke 3: 3a). He adds 'Jordan' in 4: 1. If Luke were deliberately schematizing the Jordan as the locale of John, why would he use the word but twice? Why does he omit parallel references which would have heightened this identification? Can we argue from two references, both of which are broadly paralleled in Mark and Q, that the Jordan is exclusively the region of John? Conzelmann fails to note that 'the wilderness' is even more often associated with John than the Jordan—1: 80 (by Luke); 3: 2, 4; 7: 24. Jesus also enters the wilderness (4: 2; 5: 16); here their respective locales are no longer separated. Jesus himself identifies John, not with the Jordan, but with the wilderness (7: 24). Nor can it be proved that Luke deliberately excluded Jesus from the Jordan region, for the Synoptic tradition knew of Jesus' entry into that area but once anyway (Mark 10: 1 = Matt. 19: 1), and in omitting this reference Luke omits twenty other verses besides.[3] A simple editorial excision would have sufficed.[4]

---

[1] Conzelmann, *The Theology of St Luke*, p. 20, italics mine.

[2] Note that whereas in Matt. 3: 5 'all the region about the Jordan' goes to John, implying a fixed spot for John's ministry, Luke has John going into 'all the region about the Jordan' (3: 3); i.e. John is responsible for this whole area in the same way that Jesus is responsible for Galilee and Judea (*ibid.* p. 19).

[3] William C. Robinson, Jr., review of Conzelmann's *The Theology of St Luke* in *Interpretation*, XVI, 2 (April 1962), 196.

[4] It seems more likely that Luke omitted Mark 10: 1–12 not in order to

Conzelmann argues that by excluding the locale of John from that of Jesus, Luke symbolizes the Jordan as 'the region of the old era'.[1] On the contrary, however, Luke makes the Jordan the region of fulfilment, where Isa. 40: 3–5 at long last comes to pass and where Jesus receives the Holy Spirit and the declaration of divine Sonship. It is true that Luke does more or less confine John to Jordan and the wilderness and Jesus to Galilee and Judea, but this 'schematism' appears to be traditional and need not indicate a desire to separate areas as if they were aeons![2]

Therefore we may conclude that Luke does not pursue any special geographical tendency regarding John. He locates John in the wilderness and at the Jordan because this is where tradition says John was.[3] Luke differs very little from Mark or Matthew in this respect, since all three treat the ministries of John and Jesus as separate spheres tangent only at the point of baptism. Luke records this separation faithfully, even heightening the discontinuity (3: 19 f.). The geographical motifs are thus an incidental part of Luke's over-all scheme: they emphasize the

keep Jesus out of John's territory but rather to preserve his schematization of the Jerusalem journey which has already been in progress for some nine chapters. This entire section (Luke 9: 50–18: 15) is characterized by what Streeter calls Luke's 'disuse of Mark'. From Mark 9: 41 to 10: 13 Luke abandons Mark's order and much of Mark's content and builds his so-called 'Greater Interpolation' (Streeter, *The Four Gospels*, pp. 199 ff.).

[1] *The Theology of St Luke*, p. 20.

[2] Luke's tendency to apply to Jesus the geographical hyperbole 'all Judea and Jerusalem', etc., to describe the response he received can be explained as an aspect of Luke's general tendency to limit Jesus' ministry to Palestine proper. The ministry to the Gentiles comes only after the Ascension. Creed notes that the hyperboles in 5: 17, 6: 17 and 7: 17 are all phrased in such a way as to indicate that all Palestine is represented (*St Luke*, pp. 78, 89, 104). Luke lets 'Tyre and Sidon' stand in 6: 17 because he knows (Acts 21: 3 f.) that Phoenicia is a region containing Christian communities. Nevertheless, he does not allow Jesus to enter this region, as does Mark (Conzelmann, *The Theology of St Luke*, p. 45).

[3] Note also that Luke is not loath to locate John's birthplace in Judea (1: 5, 39, 65), which, Conzelmann says, Luke jealously guards as the domain of Jesus. If Luke had such a clearly developed geographical scheme as Conzelmann thinks, he could easily have omitted those references which linked John with Judea, especially since the infancy narrative was probably added after the body of the Gospel was already complete and Luke's leading ideas were already drawn. One could wish that Conzelmann had dealt with the infancy narratives more fully.

discontinuity between the preparatory work of John and the ministry of Jesus, both of which apparently take place within the period of fulfilment (Luke 3: 4–6).

Is John excluded from the second period of salvation by Luke?

The crux of Conzelmann's argument for excluding John from the period of fulfilment is Luke 16: 16—'Ο νόμος καὶ οἱ προφῆται μέχρι 'Ιωάννου· ἀπὸ τότε ἡ βασιλεία τοῦ θεοῦ εὐαγγελίζεται καὶ πᾶς εἰς αὐτὴν βιάζεται. Conzelmann considers his interpretation of the passage so obvious that he offers no proofs in its favor. But Luke 16: 16 is one of the most debated passages in the New Testament.[1] Literally translated the passage would seem to contradict Conzelmann's interpretation: the Law and the prophets were until John (i.e. until the time of John's manifestation to Israel—1: 80; 3: 1–2); from then (the time of his manifestation) the good news of the Kingdom of God is preached, and all enter it violently. It would appear that, rather than excluding John, Luke 16: 16 dates the beginning of the epoch of salvation from the time of his manifestation.

This interpretation is corroborated by the synchronism of dates in Luke 3: 1–2. That Luke was concerned to date the beginning of the decisive period of redemptive history in terms of figures from world history is obvious; it is equally obvious that he has made *John* the inaugurator of this decisive period.[2] This exception to Conzelmann's scheme cannot be disposed of by recourse to the argument that John's inclusion in the period of the Gospel is a residuum of Luke's sources which he has not sufficiently revised, for the synchronism is wholly of Luke's

[1] Paul Minear comments on Conzelmann's use of Luke 16: 16: 'It must be said that rarely has a scholar placed so much weight on so dubious an interpretation of so difficult a logion. For him this logion determines the lines of exegesis and, in fact, the whole schematization of Luke's view of redemptive history. Strangely enough, he does not raise the question of the source for 16: 16; he does not trace the *Formgeschichte* or the *Redaktionsgeschichte* of this key verse; he does not relate it to its strange setting in Luke. . .; he does not consider possible implications of the various syntactical problems. . .' ('Luke's Use of the Birth Stories', in *Studies in Luke–Acts*, ed. by L. E. Keck and J. Louis Martyn, 1966, p. 122). Cf. also above, pp. 20 ff. and 29 ff.

[2] Conzelmann does not deal adequately with Luke 3: 1–2; at one point he even assumes that this synchronism of dates applies to *Jesus* (*The Theology of St Luke*, p. 168).

invention. In conception, Luke 3: 1 is exactly equivalent to Mark 1: 1, Luke making even more explicit than Mark that 'the beginning of the gospel' is John.

There are other passages which confirm the thesis that John is the inaugurator of the era of fulfilment. In Luke 3: 2–7 Luke inverts Mark 1: 2 f. and 1: 4, thereby accentuating the fact that Isa. 40: 3–5 is *fulfilled* by John. This is underlined by the 'therefore' in Luke 3: 7: John preaches to the multitude *because* he is the preparer of the way prophesied in Isa. 40: 3–5. Luke's arrangement of the scene makes it a programmatic fulfilment of prophecy.

Because he is already participating in the period of fulfilment even while preparing for it, John is allowed to give ethical teaching which is obviously still valid for the Christian readers of Luke's Gospel (3: 10–14). Conzelmann sought to account for this fact by arguing that Luke has regard not for John as a person, but only for his work, which is valid for successive periods.[1] But if 3: 1 f. has already placed John within the period of redemption, this forced distinction between John's person (which is relegated to the period of promise) and his work (which participates in the period of fulfilment) is altogether unnecessary.

Again, John 'preached good news (εὐηγγελίζετο) to the people' (Luke 3: 18). Conzelmann argues that the term in this context means simply 'to preach'.[2] But εὐαγγελίζομαι was by this time a technical term used to designate the whole Christian revelation centered in Jesus Christ. Apparent exceptions notwithstanding, wherever εὐαγγέλιον and εὐαγγελίζομαι appear we may assume that the Christian message of salvation is indicated, however the particular author conceives it.[3] Luke is

---

[1] *The Theology of St Luke*, p. 24. Luke's disregard for John as a person is seen in his omission of the details of his clothing, diet and death.

[2] *Ibid.* p. 23 n. 1 and pp. 221 f.

[3] Bultmann's treatment of 'evangel' (*Theology of the New Testament*, tr. by Kendrick Grobel, 1951, I, 87 f.), upon which Conzelmann depends, needs correction at several points. Εὐαγγελίζομαι may well have lost the element of 'good' news by LXX times, but as soon as Christians began to use it in connection with proof texts like Isa. 61: 1 it became *the* technical term by which the whole of the Christian message was designated. That this is already so in Mark 1: 1 is obvious. If in certain contexts its meaning is simply 'to preach', it is nonetheless *Christian* preaching which is meant. Cf.

under no pressure from any source to describe John's preaching as 'good news'. By deliberately applying the word to John's preaching Luke makes him the first preacher of the Gospel, the prototype of the Christian evangelist.[1] Likewise in 3: 3 Luke portrays John as an itinerant preacher; by so doing he accommodates him to the pattern of the Christian missionary enterprise.[2] Even John's preaching corresponds to the common primitive Christian pattern reflected in Acts:

(1) Threat of judgement;
(2) Challenge to repent;
(3) Exhortation.[3]

Because Luke has conformed John's preaching to the Christian evangelistic pattern, εὐηγγελίʒετο in 3: 18 must be allowed the full force of its use elsewhere as the key term for describing the Christian message. This 'Christianization' of John is only possible, however, because in Luke's conception he stands within Christian time.

Conzelmann rightly insists that Luke could not have John preach 'the kingdom of God' in the sense of Matt. 3: 2, for in Luke's eyes the kingdom is relegated to the distant future. But the tradition never did suggest that John preached 'the kingdom'; Matt. 3: 2 is clearly editorial. According to Christian tradition John preached the Coming One, who was Jesus (Mark 1: 2 f. par.; 7 f. par.). This is no less the case with Luke, as his addition in 3: 15 makes especially clear: John denies he is the Christ, for the one whom he precedes will be the Christ (3: 16–17). It is this preaching of the coming King, and not the coming kingdom, which Luke characterizes as the 'good news' in John's message (3: 18).

Conzelmann's assertion that Luke portrays John as the 'last of the prophets' is simply incorrect.[4] Luke adheres closely to the

G. Friedrich ('εὐαγγελίʒομαι', *TWNT*, II, 707–37) who says concerning Luke 3: 18: 'He [John]...is the evangelist...His message, then, is good news. Even as a precursor of the Messiah he is an evangelist' (p. 719).

[1] Pseudo-Bernard (*PL* 184, 997–8) had perceived this long ago: 'Behold! John, a new preacher, the first preacher of the gospel, appears to the world' (cited by André Rétif, *John the Baptist, Missionary of Christ*, 1953, p. 38).

[2] Kraeling, *John the Baptist*, p. 10.

[3] Conzelmann, *The Theology of St Luke*, p. 26.

[4] *Ibid.* p. 159 n. 1 (John is 'the last and greatest' prophet); p. 161 ('the old epoch, whose last representative was John the Baptist'); p. 167 n. 1

Q tradition in 7: 26, where he says, '"A prophet? Yes, I tell you, and *more than a prophet*"'—a statement followed by Mal. 3: 1, indicating that Luke regards John as in a *unique* sense the forerunner and messenger of Christ. Conzelmann is so intent upon emphasizing the manner in which Luke has eliminated eschatological motifs from the forerunner idea that he fails to recognize that Luke does not eliminate the forerunner idea itself, but reconceives it in terms of the delayed parousia and the present Lordship of Christ. As the forerunner of Jesus, John occupies a unique place in redemptive history, comparable neither to the prophets ('"Yes, I tell you, and *more* than a prophet"', 7: 26) nor to the apostles ('"yet he who is least in the kingdom of God is greater than he"', 7: 28). 'Thus John has a clearly defined function in the centre of the story of salvation'[1] as the prophesied preparer of the Messiah's way. As such he has an essentially higher status than the other prophets, since he already participates in that fulfilment for which they could only long (Luke 3: 4–6).

The extent to which John is significant for Christian time is seen in Acts 1: 22. The replacement for Judas among the Twelve must be 'one of the men who have accompanied us during all the time that the Lord Jesus went in and out among us, *beginning from the baptism of John* until the day when he was taken up from us'. The time span indicated marks the whole central period of salvation. It begins, however, not with 'the baptism of Jesus' or 'Jesus' baptism by John', but with the baptizing ministry of John.[2] Luke may reflect here the same tradition preserved in the Fourth Gospel, that Jesus' disciples were originally disciples of John. In any case the *arche* of the Gospel is set at

(John '...has no essentially higher status than the other prophets'); pp. 101, 185. In this connection an important correction should be made on p. 24 line 7 of the English translation, to read: 'Yet John has to be described in categories of the old epoch, as a prophet or a preacher of repentance, not in those of the new, as a "precursor", as Elijah, or as a sign of the "arrival".'

[1] *The Theology of St Luke*, p. 24, a statement which Conzelmann however empties of effect by qualification.

[2] James M. Robinson, *The Problem of History in Mark*, p. 22, understands ἀρξάμενος ἀπὸ as 'beginning with and including' John. Even if the reference were to Jesus' baptism by John, we would still have to ask why it was phrased in such a way that the whole emphasis falls upon John. U. Wilckens fails to note this (*Die Missionsreden der Apostelgeschichte*, 1961, p. 107).

Luke 3: 1 ff.; the appearance of John upon the stage of world history sets the *terminus a quo* of the church's apostolate!

All of the above evidence argues for John's inclusion in the period of fulfilment, the central epoch in the history of salvation. There are, on the other hand, passages in Luke which confirm Conzelmann's view by excluding John from the period of Jesus. The most apparent is 3: 19 f., where Luke goes to great pains to remove John from the stage before Jesus appears. Luke's motive is no doubt Christological; for the same reason as Matthew but in a different way he hesitates to portray Jesus as subordinated to John at baptism.[1] The omission of ὀπίσω μου in 3: 16 may likewise reflect embarrassment at presenting Jesus as a disciple of John.[2]

How then shall we account for the fact that John is clearly included in the era of fulfilment and yet is excluded from the period of Jesus' ministry? A slight adjustment in Conzelmann's analysis of the periods in Luke's view of redemptive history would account for all the facts. We need merely add to the three stages of the middle period of salvation a fourth: the period of preparation. The revised schematism would thus be:
  (1) The period of promise (the Law and the prophets);
  (2) The period of fulfilment (Luke 3–24):
    (*a*) The preparation—John the Baptist (3: 1–20),
    (*b*) The Galilean ministry (3: 21–9: 50),
    (*c*) The Journey to Jerusalem (9: 51–19: 27),
    (*d*) The events at Jerusalem (19: 28–24: 53),
  (3) The period of the church (The Book of Acts);
  The Parousia—The Kingdom.
Such a revision would make sense of the ambiguity surrounding John the Baptist in Luke. It preserves the independence of his ministry from that of Jesus and yet at the same time explains how it is that he participates in the fulfilment which he in-

---

[1] Note however that Acts 1: 22 undermines his whole effort.

[2] Conzelmann, *The Theology of St Luke*, p. 24, mistakenly attributes this omission to Luke's rejection of John's role as forerunner. But Luke does not mind saying that Jesus 'came after' John in a temporal sense (cf. Acts 13: 25; 19: 4; 10: 37, where he uses μετά with the accusative of Jesus' coming after John); it is only the suggestion of discipleship to John which he avoids (ὀπίσω μου being a *terminus technicus* for discipleship) (Wm. C. Robinson, Jr., 'The Theological Context for Interpreting Luke's Travel Narrative', *JBL*, LXXXIX, 1960, 30 f.).

augurates. It accounts for the fact that Luke dates the beginning of the epoch of fulfilment from John (3: 1 ff.). Above all it accounts for the actual structure of the Gospel of Luke.

The hypothesis of a preparatory stage within the period of fulfilment is confirmed by Acts 10: 36–43:

    (1) The period of promise—added as a postscript—10: 43;
    (2) The period of fulfilment—10: 36–41:
        (a) The period of preparation—John the Baptist—10: 37 b,
        (b) The Galilean ministry—10: 37 a, 38–9,
        (c) The journey to Jerusalem—10: 39 (?),
        (d) The events at Jerusalem—10: 39–41;
    (3) The period of the church—10: 41–2.

Acts 13: 17–41 also confirms this revised interpretation of John's role in *Heilsgeschichte*:

    (1) The period of promise—13: 17–22;
    (2) The period of fulfilment—13: 23–30:
        (a) The period of preparation—John the Baptist—13:24–5,
        (b) and (c) omitted,
        (d) The events at Jerusalem—13: 26–31;
    (3) The period of the church—13: 32–41.

John's ministry is clearly distinguished both from the period of promise and from the period of Jesus. It can only be explained by a separate preparatory period within the time of fulfilment.

In both Acts 10: 36 ff. and 13: 23 ff. John is mentioned only after Jesus; yet in both cases his ministry is complete before Jesus' begins.[1]

It might be objected that the addition of this period of preparation is unnecessary, since the whole first epoch of redemptive history is the preparation, Law–Prophets–Baptist. But Luke does not treat the first era as one of preparation; only John prepares the way. The Law and prophets are related to the period of Jesus as prophecy to fulfilment.[2] John's status here appears ambiguous because he participates in the fulfilment without participating in Jesus' ministry itself.

Thus in Luke's view the important fact is not the appearance

---

[1] *Contra* Wilckens, *Die Missionsreden der Apostelgeschichte*, pp. 101–5.

[2] John is never linked with the Law and prophets in the kerygmatic recitals of Acts. The Law and prophets do play a role, however, both as promise (Acts 13: 17–22) and as statutory proof after the fact (Acts 10: 43; 13: 32–7, 40–1).

of Jesus on the stage of history but rather the beginning of the period of redemption itself, which is coincident with and yet transcendent to the period of Jesus' ministry. The period neither begins with Jesus' birth (the reference to the census in 2: 1 f. does not date the beginning of redemption) nor with his baptism (3: 21 f.) nor with his public ministry (4: 16 ff.), but with John's call to prophesy (3: 1 ff.). Not Jesus, but John, initiates the time of redemption. 'He is no longer the herald of the future only, but already belongs himself to the time in which the promise is being fulfilled'; he 'stands guard at the frontier of the aeons'.[1] John is 'the figure through whom the old aeon had been brought to its end and the new aeon had been introduced'.[2] It is significant that these statements apply to the Gospels as a whole, for our study has confirmed the criticism leveled at Conzelmann by William C. Robinson, Jr.,[3] that Luke is more 'synoptic' and less 'Lukan' in regard to John than Conzelmann will allow.

(3) Conclusion

As we have seen, Luke's portrait of John the Baptist (the infancy narrative excluded) corresponds very closely to that of Q and Mark. Luke's originality lies not so much in his alteration of the traditional picture as in the way in which he has adapted John into his scheme of redemptive history. As does Q, Luke pictures John as the forerunner of the messiah, the preparer of the way, the messenger before the Lord, the preacher of judgement and repentance; and as in Q, John is not identified with Elijah nor does he bring about the restoration of all things. In these last two respects Luke shows greater dependence on the conceptions

[1] Bornkamm, *Jesus of Nazareth*, p. 51.
[2] James M. Robinson, *A New Quest of the Historical Jesus*, pp. 118 f.
[3] In a review of *The Theology of St Luke* in *Interpretation*, XVI, 2 (1962), 193–6; see also by the same author a more detailed discussion of Conzelmann's views in *The Way of the Lord: A Study of History and Eschatology in the Gospel of Luke*, doctoral dissertation at the University of Basel, 1960; now available in a revised German translation by G. Strecker, under the title *Der Weg des Herrn: Studien zur Geschichte und Eschatologie im Lukas-Evangelium, Ein Gespräch mit Hans Conzelmann* (1964). My own views were largely complete before I became aware of Robinson's work, which at many points provides independent confirmation of my discussion above. It is necessary, however, that my profound debt to Conzelmann be acknowledged.

of Q than on those of Mark. But in other respects Luke follows Mark, especially when he makes John the beginning of the Gospel at both 1 : 5 ff. and 3 : 1 ff. Even the radical segregation of John's ministry from that of Jesus (3 : 1–20) follows Mark, who also distinguishes sharply between their ministries (Mark 1 : 14 f.). Luke betrays his dependence on Mark 1 : 1 when he has John 'preach good news to the people' (3 : 18), and in both Gospels this 'good news' relates not to the imminence of the kingdom but to that of the messiah (3 : 15–17).

Luke goes beyond both Mark and Q when he portrays John as an itinerant evangelist (3 : 3, 18) and a teacher of prayer (11 : 1; 5 : 33) and ethics (3 : 10–14); but these motifs are latent in the representation of John as a prophet already developed by Q (7 : 26; 3 : 8) and betray Luke's special tendencies.

Luke's greatest innovation in the use of the traditions about John is the way he has incorporated John into his grand outline of redemptive history. Yet even here Luke follows the basic outline of Mark: that John is the 'beginning of the gospel' and that his ministry is completely set off from that of Jesus. John is the inaugurator of the fulfilment. His work as preparer of the way marks the first stage in the central epoch of salvation-history, and therefore he receives a special niche in the Christian dispensation. It is because he commands such a prominent position in the history of redemption that Luke gives him such a prominent role in his Gospel.

B. JOHN THE BAPTIST IN THE LUKAN INFANCY NARRATIVE (Luke 1–2)

Luke devotes more space to John the Baptist in the infancy narrative than he does in the rest of his Gospel.[1] And yet it is not John's message which he relates, but rather haggadic narratives about his birth. Why does he devote so much space to John in *Jesus'* nativity story?

The incontestable parallels and doublets in the birth stories of

---

[1] It is generally agreed that Luke added chapters 1 and 2 after he had already completed the body of his Gospel (Streeter, *The Four Gospels*, pp. 150, 199 ff.; F. C. Grant, *The Gospels, Their Origin and Growth*, pp. 132 f.; Feine–Behm–Kümmel, *Introduction to the New Testament*, tr. by A. J. Mattill, Jr., 1966, pp. 95 f.).

John and Jesus present a special problem. The entire narrative is dominated by a symmetry of two parts:[1]

1: 5–25. The Annunciation of the Birth of John	1: 26–38. The Annunciation of the Birth of Jesus
Presentation of the parents	Presentation of the parents
Appearance of angel (Gabriel)	Appearance of angel (Gabriel)
Zechariah is troubled	Mary is troubled
'Fear not'	'Fear not'
Announcement of the birth	Announcement of the birth
Question: How shall I know this?	*Question:* How can this be?
Response: reprimand of the angel	*Response: revelation* by the angel
Sign: Behold, you will be silent	*Sign:* Behold, your kinswoman...
Response: Zechariah is speechless due to unbelief	*Response:* Mary yields to the word of God in faith
Departure of Zechariah	Departure of the angel

1: 39–56. Parallel Greetings of the Two Mothers

1: 57–66. Birth, rejoicing, circumcision and naming of John, with accompanying wonders	2: 1–21. Birth, rejoicing, circumcision, and naming of Jesus, with accompanying wonders
1: 67–80. Greeting of child John by inspired Zechariah (Benedictus); growth of child	2: 22–40. Greeting of child Jesus by inspired Simeon and Anna (Nunc Dimittis); growth of child

2: 41–52. Proof of surpassing significance of Jesus by his behavior in Temple

If the entire narrative were straightforward history then these parallels would present no problem. But if this is not the case (and few argue that it is)[2] we are apparently left with two alternatives: either the Baptist material was prior and the church has followed it in producing the story of Jesus' birth, or the account of the birth of Jesus was prior and the infancy of John has been conformed to it. The majority of scholars seems in-

[1] The following analysis is a conflation of those set forth by Dibelius, *Johannes der Täufer*, p. 67, and R. Laurentin, *Structure et théologie de Luc I–II* (1957), pp. 32 f.

[2] Even those who find a large residuum of history here consider the parallels to be a stylized schematism dictated by the theology of the editors.

clined to the view that a Baptist nativity is the earliest source, and that Christians adapted it and subordinated it to a parallel nativity of Jesus patterned after that of John.[1]

(1) *The Theory of a Baptist Source behind Luke 1*

Several of the North Italian Latin versions ascribe the Magnificat to Elizabeth.[2] This MS variant suggests that the Magnificat may have originally belonged to a 'Baptist Nativity' and has been adapted to Mary by Christians. Elsewhere in Luke 1 scholars have noted what Kraeling calls the absence of 'the common Gospel tendency to subordinate John to Jesus and to regard him as Jesus' Forerunner'.[3] John plays so exalted a role that a Baptist milieu of composition seems to be indicated. John will 'turn many of the sons of Israel to the Lord their God', he will 'make ready for the Lord a people prepared' (1: 16 f.)—for the Lord, not the messiah. John's birth is the signal that the day of redemption *has* come and that *he* is the one chosen to give the knowledge of salvation to God's people (1: 68–79).[4] He is

---

[1] First proposed by D. Völter, *Theol. Tijdschrift* (1896), this thesis has been developed by Baldensperger, *Der Prolog des vierten Evangeliums* (1898), p. 135; J. R. Wilkinson, *A Johannine Document in the First Chapter of St Luke's Gospel* (1902); Völter again in *Die Geburt des Täufers Johannes und Jesus nach Lukas* (1911), pp. 209 f.; M. Dibelius, *Johannes der Täufer* (1911), pp. 67–77; C. R. Bowen, 'John the Baptist in the New Testament', *AJT*, XVI (1912), 90–106; E. Norden, *Die Geburt des Kindes* (1924), pp. 102–5; R. Eisler, *The Messiah Jesus and John the Baptist* (1928–30); M. Goguel, *Jean-Baptiste* (1928), pp. 70 ff.; H. Schonfield, *The Lost 'Book of the Nativity of John'* (1929); R. Bultmann, *Die Geschichte der synoptischen Tradition* (1931), pp. 320 f.; G. Erdmann, *Die Vorgeschichten des Lukas- und Matthäusevangeliums* (1932); Dibelius again in *Jungfrauensohn und Krippenkind* (1932), p. 10 (republished in *Botschaft und Geschichte*, I, 1953, 8), and *From Tradition to Gospel* (1934); E. Lohmeyer, *Johannes der Täufer* (1932); W. Bauer, *Das Johannesevangelium* (1933), p. 16; C. Kraeling, *John the Baptist*, pp. 16 ff.; Ph. Vielhauer, *ZThK*, XLIX (1952), 255–72; J. Lambertz, *Wiss. Zeitsch. d. Univ. Leipzig* (1952/3), 80; Paul Winter, *ZNTW*, XLVII (1956), 217–42 and *ATR*, XL (1958), 257–64; W. R. Farmer, 'John the Baptist', *Interpreter's Dictionary of the Bible*, II, 955–62; H. Thyen, 'Βάπτισμα Μετανοίας εἰς ἄφεσιν ἁμαρτιῶν', in *Zeit und Geschichte: Rudolf Bultmann zum 80. Geburtstag*, ed. by E. Dinkler (1964), pp. 97–125.

[2] a. b. 1*, Irenaeus 235 (but not in 185), Niceta, and the Latin of Origen (Jerome).

[3] *John the Baptist*, p. 17.

[4] *Ibid.*

called 'great' (μέγας), an ascription which commentators variously understand as hellenistic ('divine') or Jewish ('man of God').[1] Some, who regard 1: 67–80 as part of the original Baptist source, argue that John is the 'horn of salvation' of the 'house of His servant David', and insist that John's disciples regarded him as the Davidic messiah. External attestation of this view is sought in the *Clementine Recognitions* 1, 60, where 'one of John's disciples declared John to be the messiah and not Jesus', and in John 1: 19 ff. and Luke 3: 15, where John is made to say explicitly that he is not the messiah.

This hypothesis of a non-Christian Baptist document behind Luke 1 has proved so effective in reconstructing the later history of the Baptist movement that many scholars treat it as a foregone conclusion.

Let us examine the evidence for this 'Lost Nativity of John'.

(*a*) *Are there stylistic and linguistic differences between the John and Jesus sections in Luke 1–2?* If it could be shown that the Baptist narratives possess distinctive literary characteristics, this might establish a presumption in favor of their separate origin. There are strong reasons for believing that the traditions underlying Luke 1–2 originated in Judea, in Hebrew or Aramaic:

(1) The abundance of Semitisms,[2]

---

[1] Dibelius, *Botschaft und Geschichte*, I, 4.

[2] R. Laurentin, *Structure et théologie de Luc I–II*, pp. 12 f., notes that:

(1) retranslation into Hebrew is possible and reads naturally;

(2) original mistranslation would account for certain obscurities, notably 'city' in 1: 39, which Sahlin suggests is a mistranslation of מדינה, province;

(3) lyrical passages possess a regular metre in Hebrew;

(4) a large number of assonances appear in the Hebrew, i.e. 1: 17 and 76, where John goes *before the face* (לְפְנֵי) of God *to prepare* (לְפַנּוֹת) his way; 1: 56 'stayed' (וַתֵּשֶׁב)...'returned' (וַתָּשָׁב); 2: 11 'a Savior (מוֹשִׁיעַ) who is Christ' (מָשִׁיחַ);

(5) word-plays in Hebrew on the names of the principal characters (cf. below, pp. 64, 67, and Laurentin, 'Traces d'allusions etymologiques en Lc. 1–2', *Biblica*, xxxvii, 1956, 435–56; xxxviii, 1957, 1–23).

Cf. also Paul Winter's several articles, especially 'Some Observations on the Language in the Birth and Infancy Stories of the Third Gospel', *NTS*, I (1954–5), 111–21; 'Two Notes on Lk. 1–2...', *Studia Theologica*, VII (1953), 158–65. For a contrary view see Nigel Turner, 'The Relation of Luke I and II to Hebraic Sources and to the Rest of Luke–Acts', *NTS*, II, 2 (1955), 100–9; P. Benoit, 'L'Enfance de Jean-Baptiste selon Luc I', *NTS*, III (1956–7), 169–94.

(2) the accurate reflection of Palestinian customs and practices which would be unfamiliar to a Gentile and inaccessible in the LXX,[1]

(3) the unusual number of colloquialisms (suggesting popular or folk, not literary origin),[2] and

(4) the fact that the perspective seems to be limited to Israel.[3]

Nowhere are these semitic and Palestinian touches more apparent than in the account of John's birth. Even the style there is rougher.[4] But such evidence does not necessarily argue for separate origins for the Jesus and John traditions, since the traditions about Jesus would naturally have received more liturgical use by the church and would have been subjected to greater refinements. The presence of Semitisms indicates that Luke used Hebrew traditions, but their frequency in any given section cannot be used as an argument for a Baptist source since these Semitisms also appear in the traditions about Jesus.

(b) *Was the Magnificat (Luke 1: 46–55) originally ascribed to Elizabeth?* Many scholars are convinced that it was. F. C. Burkitt's approach is representative.[5] The textual evidence for the reading 'Elizabeth' at 1: 46a is really so slim that Burkitt

[1] Cf. Winter, 'The Cultural Background of the Narrative in Luke I and II', *Jewish Quarterly Review*, XLV–XLVI (1954–6), 159–69. He cites 1: 5 ('the course of Abijah'), 1: 9 (drawing lots), 1: 9 ff. (burning incense), 1: 11 (the angel of the presence), 1: 58 ff. (the fête after John's birth), 2: 8 (the watch tower at Bethlehem), 2: 37 (night and day as the Jewish manner of reckoning time).

[2] Dibelius, *Johannes der Täufer*, p. 68, comments that rediscovery of the original language is complicated by the presence of what may simply be 'folk-language'.

[3] Laurentin, *Structure et théologie*, p. 102. Allusions to the Gentiles in 2: 32 and perhaps 2: 10 and 31 are no exceptions, for what is involved is the nationalistic notion that the nations will see the light of Israel, not that they themselves will be saved. In other passages the scope of salvation is explicitly limited to Israel (1: 14, 16, 32, 33, 54, 55, 65, 68, 69, 71–4, 77; 2: 25, 32b, 34, 38, etc.).

Note also the absence of conflict between Jewish and Gentile Christians, law and grace, and especially between national and religious hopes—all of which suggest an early Palestinian milieu.

[4] V. Taylor, 'The Gospel of Luke', *Interpreter's Dictionary of the Bible*, III, 185.

[5] 'Who Spoke the Magnificat?', *JTS*, VII (1905–6), 220–7.

rules out the possibility that it was original.[1] He conjectures therefore that καὶ εἶπεν ('and *she* said') originally stood alone in Luke's recension of 1: 46*a* and that later Christian copyists, puzzled by the ambiguity of the reference, supplied 'Mary' or 'Elizabeth' according to which they thought was the more appropriate. The reading 'Elizabeth' in these Latin MSS thus represents an exegetical gloss which in time found its way into the text. But who then says the Magnificat? Hitherto Elizabeth has been speaking. If Luke had intended to change the speaker to Mary, why would he have done it so ineffectively? Furthermore, 1: 56 concludes with the words, 'And Mary remained with *her*'. If Mary had just been speaking, would the text not have read, 'And *she* remained with Elizabeth'? Burkitt concludes therefore that Luke understood Elizabeth to be the speaker of the Magnificat. καὶ εἶπεν is a familiar Lukan phrase, having been suggested here by its prototype in the Song of Hannah, which is the basis of the entire Magnificat. Thus exactly as in I Sam. 1–2, Elizabeth speaks to someone else about her child and then lapses into pious meditation, καὶ εἶπεν marking in both contexts not a change of speaker but rather a change in the mode of speech. True, Burkitt admits, the ascription of the Magnificat to Elizabeth leaves almost nothing to Mary, but a similar pattern is followed when Mary confronts Simeon and says nothing. Likewise the situation of Elizabeth seems more appropriate to that of Hannah in I Samuel than to that of Mary, and Luke 1: 48 (the ταπείνωσιν τῆς δούλης) refers directly to Hannah's prayer in I Sam. 1: 11 (τὴν ταπείνωσιν τῆς δούλης— LXX). The allusion to the Song of Hannah would also explain the references in the Magnificat to dynasties and thrones, the rich and the poor (Luke 1: 51–3; I Sam. 2: 4–10). And finally,

---

[1] 'Such a consensus of authority [for the reading "Mary"] is practically fatal to the claim of "Elizabeth" to be considered the original reading. Yet if "Mary" were genuine the actual occurrence of "Elizabeth" in the European branch of the Old Latin would be inexplicable' (*ibid.* p. 221). Loisy first suggested, under the pen-name of François Jacobé, that 'Elizabeth' was the original reading (in *L'enseignement biblique*, 1893, pp. 35–6). A. Durand countered that καὶ εἶπεν originally stood alone in 1: 46*a* and that due to its ambiguity was corrected by some to Μαριάμ and by others to Ἐλισάβετ (*Revue Biblique*, VII, 1898, 74–7). See Laurentin, 'Traces d'allusions étymologiques en Luc 1–2', *Biblica*, XXXVIII (1957), 19–23 ('Note-annexe 2: La controverse sur l'attribution du "Magnificat"') for a complete bibliography on the controversy.

Burkitt finds an allusion to John the Baptist in Luke 1: 50 and 54 ('mercy'), for John's name means 'Yahweh has shown mercy'. If all this were true, then there would be good grounds for arguing that the Magnificat originally derived from a Baptist source, if on other grounds we knew that such a source existed. Yet the Magnificat does not apply messianic titles to John, nor is there anything in the hymn more appropriate to Baptist than to Christian circles.

But is the attribution of the Magnificat to Elizabeth correct? René Laurentin has discovered several instances of paronomasia in the Hebrew substratum of the infancy narratives, especially in the canticles.[1] In the first line of the Magnificat he finds a word-play on the name of Mary:

וַתֹּאמֶר מִרְיָם מְרִימָה (or מֵרִים) נַפְשִׁי יהוה

The second line possibly refers to Jesus (יֵשׁוּעַ) in the phrase 'my Savior' (יִשְׁעִי), though this allusion is by no means as certain (but cf. 2: 11, 1: 69 and 2: 30). Then in 1: 54b–55a, Zechariah, John and Elizabeth are all alluded to in a single phrase:[2]

to remember—לִזְכֹּר—Zechariah (זְכַרְיָה—Yahweh remembers)
the mercies—חֲנוֹת—John (יוֹחָנָן—Yahweh has shown mercy)
which he spoke—כַּאֲשֶׁר נִשְׁבַּע—Elizabeth (אֱלִישֶׁבַע—God has sworn)

In only a few cases are any of the words used in these allusions found elsewhere in the Gospels. Laurentin demonstrates the popularity of such word-plays in the Old Testament and intertestamental literature and creates a strong presumption in favor of his analysis. The case for the Magnificat is strengthened by other allusions in Luke 1–2 which are even more transparent.

If Laurentin's argument can be sustained, then it offers a solution to the problem of the ascription of the Magnificat. The allusion to Mary in 1: 46b is virtually a signature and clearly indicates that Mary is the speaker. Why then the ambiguity of καὶ εἶπεν? Laurentin points out that in Hebrew the word-play has all the appearance of a dittography:

---

[1] Laurentin, 'Traces d'allusions étymologiques en Luc 1–2', *Biblica*, XXXVII, 435–56; XXXVIII, 1–23.

[2] *Ibid.* XXXVIII, 3. 'Spoke' (ἐλάλησεν) implies an oath; cf. 1: 73 and below, p. 67 n. 4.

וַתֹּאמֶר מרים מרימ(ה)

and that apparently the first מרים was dropped even before the tradition reached Luke.[1] Christian copyists subsequently supplied Μαριάμ or Ἐλισάβετ as they saw fit.

Seen in this light, then, the Magnificat bears every mark of Christian composition *ad hoc*.[2] The strange references to kings and thrones are due to dependence on I Sam. 2, while the awkwardness of 1 : 54 f. is due to the etymological allusions themselves. The reference to 'the low estate of his handmaiden' in 1 : 48 and 52 refers to the humility of Mary in 1 : 38, not to the barrenness of Elizabeth.[3] The story of Hannah suggested itself as the basis of composition because it is the classic story of childbirth in the Old Testament, and its contents comport perfectly with the wonder felt in the entire infancy narrative: that the Savior is born, not to a queen in a castle, but to a 'handmaid' of 'low estate' such as Mary.

There is therefore no convincing evidence that Baptists ever employed the Magnificat in an alleged 'Nativity of John'.

(*c*) *Is the Benedictus (1 : 68–79) a Baptist Hymn?* There is little agreement on this question among proponents of the 'Baptist source' theory. Some deny Baptists used it,[4] others say all but 1 : 76–7 or 79 is Baptist,[5] others say the whole of it is Baptist.[6] Those who believe that the Benedictus derives from a Baptist source argue that its messianic ascriptions originally applied to John, and use it as evidence for the existence of a John-cult.

The evidence, however, does not support such a claim. As it stands, the Benedictus naturally falls into two parts, 1 : 68–75 and 1 : 76–9, the first part referring to the Davidic messiah, the second to John's role as the messiah's forerunner. The use of the

---

[1] It thus remains a possibility that Luke understood 'Elizabeth' (cf. 1 : 56) even though the original tradition ascribed the Magnificat to 'Mary'!

[2] This is Harnack's judgement ('Das Magnificat der Elisabet [Luke 1 : 46–55] nebst einigen Bemerkungen zu Luk. 1 und 2', in *Studien zur Geschichte des Neuen Testaments und der Alten Kirche*, 1, 84 f.).

[3] Dibelius, *Botschaft und Geschichte*, 1, 14.

[4] Dibelius, in all works cited.

[5] Kraeling, *John the Baptist*, pp. 166 ff.; Winter, 'Magnificat and Benedictus—Maccabean Hymns?', *Bulletin of the John Rylands Library*, XXXVII (1954), 328–47.

[6] Goguel, *Jean-Baptiste*, p. 74; P. Vielhauer, 'Das Benedictus des Zacharias', *ZThK*, XLIX (1952), 255–72.

aorist in *vv.* 68–75 (nine times) and the future in *vv.* 76–9 (three times) underlines this division. These aorists only *appear* to be 'prophetic aorists' (i.e. verbs which speak of a future event as if it has already been realized); they are in fact simple aorists[1] and attest to the faith of the church: in Jesus, God has already accomplished all that he promised by the prophets. The bipartite division is dictated by theological necessity, for John's significance is altogether contingent upon that of Jesus. Therefore Zechariah must dwell on the salvation wrought by Jesus as prelude to the role played by John in this salvation. This temporal reversal exactly corresponds to the Synoptic judgement (Mark 1: 7 par.) which finds its logical development in John 1: 30—'after me comes a man who ranks before me'.

No one would deny that Luke and the Christian redactors of the Benedictus thought that all of its messianic ascriptions applied to Jesus. The only question is, did they originally apply to John? There is no evidence that they did. Luke 1: 76 f. conforms to the Christian view of John as prophet and forerunner, whose proclamation of forgiveness prepares Israel with the knowledge of how it shall be saved.[2] Several elements are missing: judgement, repentance, the Day of the Lord, baptism.[3] Only those elements are incorporated which contribute toward a selective Christian portrait of John.

John is 'prophet of the Most High', which is to be understood as 'a prophet of God' and not as 'the prophet who *precedes* God'. This interpretation is confirmed by 1: 32, where Jesus is called 'Son of the Most High', i.e. Son of God. John will 'go before the Lord to prepare his ways', an unmistakable allusion to Mal. 3: 1 and Isa. 40: 3, conflated in somewhat the same manner as in Mark 1: 2 f. The Old Testament allusion determines the use of 'Lord' here, but the context makes it clear that Jesus is meant. Consistently throughout Luke 1 and 2 titles and

[1] Benoit, 'L'Enfance de Jean-Baptiste selon Luc I', *NTS*, III (1956–7), 186.

[2] Cf. Luke 3: 4–6, where Luke alone quotes Isa. 40: 4–5 in regard to the work of John, concluding with the line, 'all flesh shall *see* the *salvation* of God'.

[3] Repentance, however, has already been implied by 1: 16–17. The absence of 'baptism' in a 'Baptist' source would be inexplicable (Benoit, 'L'Enfance de Jean-Baptiste', *op. cit.* p. 190).

attributes of God are applied to Jesus, i.e. 'horn of salvation',[1] 'light'[2] and even 'Savior' (2: 11). John precedes the 'dayspring from on high', an allusion to Mal. 4: 2 understood by Christians to refer to Jesus (cf. Eph. 5: 14; Matt. 4: 16).[3]

That the Benedictus is from its very inception a Jewish-Christian hymn is suggested by the allusions to Jesus imbedded in it. Luke 1: 69 says that God 'has raised up' (ἤγειρεν) a horn of salvation from the house of David, a phrase with many parallels in Acts (cf. 2: 24, 32; 3: 15, 22, 26; 4: 10; 5: 30; 13: 30, 34, 37). The early church undoubtedly saw here a reference to the resurrection of Jesus. Even more revealing are the word-plays in the canticle. John preaches the knowledge of 'salvation' (יְשׁוּעָה), which the reader perceives to be knowledge about *Jesus* (יֵשׁוּעַ). Laurentin argues that such word-plays are not fortuitous, for in the Nunc dimittis Simeon says, 'mine eyes have seen thy salvation' (יְשׁוּעָתֶךָ) as he holds the infant Jesus (יֵשׁוּעַ) in his arms.[4] John is here again conformed to the greatest/least role so typical of his treatment throughout the Gospels: John

---

[1] 1: 69; in the Old Testament twice—Ps. 18: 2 = II Sam. 22: 3, in both cases meaning 'Yahweh'; cf. Laurentin, *Structure et théologie*, p. 125.

[2] 1: 79 and 2: 32; in the Old Testament usually an emanation from Yahweh—Isa. 2: 5; Job 29: 3; Isa. 60: 19 f. (*ibid.* p. 123).

[3] Vielhauer, *op. cit.* p. 266, concedes that ἀνατολὴ ἐξ ὕψους is a messianic ascription but applies it to John. But the point of 76–9 is that John is the forerunner of this ἀνατολὴ ἐξ ὕψους. Vielhauer would have been more consistent had he argued that the ἀνατολὴ was God himself, and that John was God's forerunner; but the evidence would not allow that either.

[4] *Structure et théologie*, p. 126; 'Traces d'allusions étymologiques en Luc 1–2', *Biblica*, XXXVIII (1957). Laurentin finds extensive word-plays in both the Benedictus and Magnificat (see above, p. 64). In the Benedictus he finds:

1: 69a—'he has raised up a horn of salvation' קֶרֶן (Mary?) מֶרִים יְשׁוּעָה (Jesus?).

1: 71—σωτηρίαν is in apposition to 'horn of salvation' in 1: 69 and repeats the allusion to Jesus.

1: 72–73—'...the mercy'—הָחֹנֵן (John—יוֹחָנָן) '...to remember'—לִזְכֹּר (Zechariah—זְכַרְיָה) '...the oath which he swore'—הַשְּׁבוּעָה אֲשֶׁר נִשְׁבַּע (Elizabeth—אֱלִישֶׁבַע).

1: 78—'mercy' (John) immediately precedes the 'day-spring' (Jesus). Not all of these allusions have equal weight, but some are more probable and raise the presumption in favor of the others. The presence of allusions to John and his parents in both canticles suggests that the songs were originally composed with both Jesus and John in mind. Cf. also J. Rendel Harris, 'Mary or Elizabeth?', *ET*, XLI (1929–30), 266 f.

merely preaches the knowledge of salvation, he himself is not the instrument of salvation (the 'horn of salvation', 1: 69); he is prophet of the Most High, not Son of the Most High; he goes *before* the Lord, he is not himself called 'Lord' (1: 43; 2: 11).

The most telling argument against a Baptist origin for the Benedictus is the allusion to the Davidic lineage of the 'horn of salvation' referred to in the first strophe of the canticle (*vv.* 68–71). If the entire Benedictus originally referred to John, then he would have to be of Davidic stock (1: 69*b*); but we know nothing of John's Davidic descent. No later tradition describes him thus. Against it we have the testimony of the infancy narrative itself that John was doubly anchored in the priestly line. This would make Davidic lineage impossible. On the other hand we have excellent grounds for believing that Jesus was of the house of David (Rom. 1: 1–4; Mark 10: 47; 12: 35 ff., etc.). It follows that Luke 1: 69 at no time referred to 'Johanan ben Zecharias'.[1]

We must conclude, therefore, that there is no basis whatever for arguing that the Benedictus was originally a Baptist hymn. It is an unashamedly Christian hymn which spares only two verses to John.[2] Zechariah can rejoice in his son's birth only because the messiah has been conceived. John's birth is significant only because of Jesus'—a theological statement which might be said to have a degree of historical validity as well.

(*d*) *Is there a Baptist source behind Luke 1: 5–25 and 57–66?* The

---

[1] C. H. H. Scobie, *John the Baptist*, p. 55, asserts that the phrase 'from the house of his servant David' in 1: 69*b* is 'almost certainly to be excluded as a later gloss' since it 'spoils' the metre of the psalm when the original Hebrew is reconstructed. This assertion is particularly difficult to assess since he presents no evidence to support it. Apparently he is following R. A. Aytoun, 'The Ten Lukan Hymns of the Nativity in Their Original Language', *JTS*, XVIII (1917), 274–88, who nevertheless regards the hymn as alluding to a Davidic redeemer (p. 284—'the Branch has visited us'). Both M. Black (*An Aramaic Approach to the Gospels and Acts*, 2nd ed., 1954, p. 113) and Streeter (*The Four Gospels*, p. 266) regard 1: 69*b* as integral to the context. Scobie's rejection of 1: 69*b* appears to stem from his belief that the Benedictus was originally a Baptist poem, in which Davidic references obviously had no place. But even if 1: 69*b* were omitted as a Christian interpolation, 1: 69*a* would still refer to a Davidic redeemer-figure, since 'horn' is a frequent designation for the anointed king (I Sam. 2: 10; Ps. 89: 20–4; Ps. 132: 13, 17—'There I will make a horn to sprout for David'; Ezek. 29: 21—'On that day I will cause a horn to spring forth to the house of Israel').

[2] M. D. Goulder and M. L. Sanderson, 'St Luke's Genesis', *JTS*, VIII, I (April 1957), 21.

only clue to such a source would be messianic ascriptions applied to John which ordinarily were reserved for Jesus by the church. Let us examine the evidence. John is of priestly stock. He will be 'great' before the Lord, ascetic, endowed with the Spirit as a prophet from birth. His role will be that of the messenger of Malachi: to preach repentance and to make ready for the Lord a people prepared (1: 14–17). Here, as in 1: 76 f., only those aspects which qualify John as the prophetic forerunner are retained. Virtually every detail is 'Synoptic': his asceticism (Luke 7: 33 Q), his function as the prophet like Elijah of Mal. 3–4 (Mark 1: 2), his role as forerunner and preparer of the way (Mark 1: 2 f.), his prophetic office (Luke 7: 26 Q). The very fact that John's birth precedes that of Jesus shows that John is still considered to be 'the beginning of the gospel of Jesus Christ', just as he is in Mark 1: 1, even though his 'coming' has now been pushed back from baptism to birth. Thus John's conception can be proclaimed by the angel as 'good news' (Luke 1: 19—εὐαγγελίσασθαί). Even the apparent Semitism ἑτοιμάσαι . . . κατεσκευασμένον is Synoptic, representing a conflation of Isa. 40: 3 (ἑτοιμάσατε, Luke 3: 4) and Mal. 3: 1 (κατασκευάσει, Luke 7: 27)—a conflation, it will be noted, of exactly the same nature as Mark 1: 2–3.[1]

Are there then any non-Synoptic notes? John is called μέγας ἐνώπιον κυρίου (1: 15); some have argued that the word μέγας here is a designation of divinity and indicates that John was worshipped by his followers. It is true that Luke understands μέγας to designate divinity (cf. Acts 8: 10, where Simon Magus is sarcastically called 'Great'—μεγάλη), but only when it is used without qualification. John is 'great before the Lord'; but Jesus is unqualifiedly 'great' (μέγας) and therefore can be called 'Son of the Most High' (Luke 1: 32).[2] Again, John will prepare the

[1] Benoit, 'L'Enfance de Jean-Baptiste selon Luc 1', *NTS*, III (1956–7), 180 f. Benoit refers to the portrait of John the Baptist in Luke 1 as 'a Synoptic orchestration' aided by biblical and Lukan themes. Note the number of Lukanisms in 1: 14–17, notably καὶ αὐτός, ἐνώπιον, προελεύσεται, and the coupling of πνεῦμα and δύναμις (*ibid.* p. 181).

[2] Laurentin, *Structure et théologie*, pp. 36 f. For 'great before God' as meaning simply 'man of God', cf. Sir. 48: 22 and Gen. 10: 9; for 'great' alone used of a man implying greatness, cf. II Sam. 19: 32; Lev. 19: 15; Esther 10: 3. As an attribute of God, 'great' is used in Tobit 12: 22; Ps. 47: 2; 77: 13; 86: 10; 96: 4; etc. (*ibid.* p. 36 nn. 3–5).

people 'for the Lord', not Jesus (1: 16, 17, 76). Does this indicate that this was a Baptist hymn to John, the forerunner of God? So many have argued. But the use of 'the Lord' here is simply dictated by the scriptural allusions (Mal. 3: 1; Isa. 40: 3). Either God or Jesus can be inferred (except in 1: 16), for in Luke's view God is the principal actor in history, even where his chosen instruments are concerned.[1]

At every other point the picture of John in Luke 1: 5–25 conforms to that in Mark and Q. John's carefully qualified role as forerunner reflects, not an attempt to subordinate him to Jesus in the interest of anti-Baptist polemic (for their relationship remains the same even in this new context),[2] but rather a stage in the evolution of Christology as 'the beginning of the Gospel' is pushed back from Resurrection to Baptism to Birth to Pre-Existence.[3] The most remarkable fact from the point of view of our study is that John should be deemed worthy to participate in this Christological development at all, and that a Gospel about Jesus Christ should devote so much space to the birth of John.

(e) *Are there traces of a Baptist community in Luke 1?* This is a fair question to ask of the source, for it also unwittingly reflects at every point the faith and life of the church.[4] But there is not the slightest reference to a Baptist community. What John must do he can do alone; and what he has done is done once for all time. Luke 1 envisions no continuing 'Johannite ministry'. In the prophecies about John's mission, we find nothing about his gathering a community of the baptized, a remnant of wheat snatched out of the fire, a people baptized in Holy Spirit (or

[1] 'God' is used twenty times in Luke 1–2, 'Lord' (referring to God) twenty-four to twenty-six times, 'Most High' three times; total, forty-seven to forty-nine times. Compare this with 'Jesus' (five times), 'Mary' (twelve times), 'John' (three times). (Cf. also Wm. C. Robinson, *The Way of the Lord*, p. 113.)

[2] A. Schlatter, *Das Evangelium des Lukas* (1931), p. 178, remarks that there is no sign in Luke 1 of discord between John and Jesus or between John's disciples and the apostles.

[3] This process, Benoit remarks ('L'Enfance de Jean-Baptiste selon Luc I', *NTS*, III (1956–7), 192), is not the progressive creation of a myth but rather the progressive apprehension of a mystery. We would ask, what is the difference?

[4] Cf. especially Paul Minear, 'The Interpreter and the Nativity Stories', *Theology Today*, VII, 3 (1950), 358–75.

anticipating such a baptism), a community bearing fruits worthy of repentance, which follows the ethical exhortations of Luke 3: 10–14 and which uses a set form of prayer (Luke 11: 1). The only practices this community might have left stamped on the narrative would be asceticism (1: 15) and repentance and forgiveness preaching (1: 16 f., 77). But these characteristics already belonged to John, so that they cannot serve as evidence for the practices of his community. Yet these very prophecies do look forward to the church, i.e. the church saw itself prefigured and prepared for in the birth of the Baptist. The λαός John prepared (1: 17) is the ἐκκλησία.

In conclusion, then, we have found no evidence that there was behind Luke 1 a 'Baptist Nativity' which attributed messianic titles to John. There are only Baptist traditions, probably brought over to the church by former Baptists.[1] Or, to state it perhaps more accurately, the church possessed these traditions from the very beginning by virtue of the fact that it was itself an outgrowth of the Baptist movement.[2] In the church these traditions continued to develop, until at some point they were worked into artful symmetry with the traditions of Jesus' birth. This parallelism is the artistic expression of the theological conviction of the authors, that through *both* men God has worked the redemption of Israel. This hypothesis would explain why John is given so much space and devotion in these chapters: by assigning John so lofty a role in God's redemptive purpose his former disciples have discovered the meaning of both their past and present, and have, in a sense, vicariously converted their former master to Jesus Christ.[3]

Hitherto only two alternatives seemed possible regarding the infancy traditions in Luke: either the Baptist material was prior and the church imitated it in constructing the nativity of Jesus;

[1] Barton suggested this in his revision of Buzy's *Life of S. John the Baptist* (1933), pp. 21 f., as did Kraeling, *John the Baptist*, p. 175. The studies of Harnack (*Luke the Physician*) and Benoit ('L'Enfance de Jean-Baptiste selon Luc I', *op. cit.*, pp. 169 ff.), however, still argue for a large role for Luke himself in the shaping of the narrative.

[2] So correctly—and perhaps only in this respect correct—C. A. Bernoulli, *Johannes der Täufer und die Urgemeinde* (1918), pp. 104, 140 f.

[3] The tradition that several of the Twelve were former Baptists (Acts 1: 22; John 1: 35 ff.) is very attractive, and would explain the abruptness with which the disciples follow Jesus in Mark 1: 16 ff.

or else the account of Jesus' birth was prior and the birth of John was conformed to it. Our analysis has shown neither alternative to be true. Instead a third has emerged: the stories of Jesus and John developed *together*, from the very beginning, as an indissoluble unity, born of the devotion of the church to these two who had, each in his own way, mediated their salvation.

(2) *The Theory of a Two-Messiahs Concept behind Luke 1–2*

Because John occupies such a crucial position in the infancy narrative, a further question suggests itself: Is it possible that behind the 'forerunner/Christ' concept of the relationship between John and Jesus, there lies an earlier 'two-messiahs' belief in which John plays the part of the priestly messiah, the messiah of Aaron?

The Dead Sea Scrolls have now confirmed the view that certain sectarian Jews expected two messiahs, one a priestly messiah, the messiah of Aaron, the other a Davidic or kingly messiah, the messiah of Israel.[1] Most scholars still contend, however, that the New Testament knows nothing of the expectation of two messiahs.[2] Yet few writers have asked whether the parallelism between John and Jesus in the infancy narrative may have originated out of just such a belief. Schonfield had suggested as early as 1929 that 'in the first two chapters of the *Gospel of Luke* we have a composite document made up of the birth stories of two Messiahs, John and Jesus, though it is inten-

---

[1] The texts most frequently cited are CDC 12: 23; 14: 19; 19: 10 f.; 20: 1; Test. Reub. 6: 7–12; Test. Lev. 2: 11; 4: 5, 16; 6: 15; 4: 3; 8: 14; 17: 2–3; 18: 2–14; Test. Sim. 7: 2; Test. Dan 5: 4, 7, 10; Test. Gad 8: 1; Test. Jos. 19: 11; Test. Judah 12: 4; 15: 2–3; 17: 3, 5–6; 22: 2–3; 21: 2–5; 25: 1–2; Test. Iss. 5: 7; Test. Napht. 5: 3–5; Test. Sim. 5: 5–6; 1QS 6: 4–6; 9: 10–11; 1QSa 2: 12–20. (Cf. K. G. Kuhn, 'The Two Messiahs of Aaron and Israel', *The Scrolls and the New Testament*, ed. K. Stendahl, pp. 54–64.)

Scholars are not unanimous in interpreting the evidence. The literature is voluminous. Cf. the discussions of John Priest, 'Mebaqqer, Paqid, and the Messiah', *JBL*, LXXXI, 1 (1962), 55–61; and his 'The Messiah and the Meal in 1QSa', *JBL*, LXXXII, 1 (1963), 95–100; G. Friedrich, 'Beobachtungen zur messianischen Hohepriestererwartung in den Synoptikern', *ZThK*, LIII (1956), 270 ff.; R. B. Laurin, 'The Problem of Two Messiahs in the Qumran Scrolls', *RQ*, IV, 13, 1 (1963), 39–52; and Kurt Schubert, *The Dead Sea Community*, pp. 113–21.

[2] K. G. Kuhn, 'The Two Messiahs of Aaron and Israel', *op. cit.* p. 63.

tionally made to appear as if the former were only the fore-runner of the latter'; and that 'the messianic expectation which lies behind the nativity stories of John the Baptist is that of the Priestly Messiah'.[1] Laurentin has recently developed this theory further.[2]

In the first place, Laurentin observes that Jesus' role as Davidic messiah and king (i.e. messiah of Israel) is nowhere more pronounced than in Luke 1–2. He is the son of David by birth, the first-born of the Davidic Joseph (1: 27, 32, 69; 2: 4, 11). To him will be given the throne of David forever (1: 32 f.). He will gather together the twelve tribes of Israel in remembrance of the Abrahamic covenant (1: 54 f.).[3] The benefits of his office extend only to Israel. He reigns only over 'the house of Jacob' (1: 33), he brings deliverance only to 'Israel' (1: 54, 68, 73; 2: 25, 32, 34) and redemption only to 'Jerusalem' (2: 38). The Gentiles will see his light and be dazzled thereby (2: 32 a); but we are not told that they will be saved. Instead only the vindication of Israel seems to be contemplated (2: 32 b). For as a result of his rule oppressive kings and nations will be cast down and Israel will be elevated (1: 51–5, 71, 74).[4] The views reflected here are apparently those of Jewish-Christians who as yet feel no tension between their political and their religious hopes, and who still consider the promise of the land to Abraham to be binding, literally (1: 55, 73). The extent to which this

---

[1] The Lost 'Book of the Nativity of John', pp. 26 and 48; so also H. Thyen, 'Βάπτισμα μετανοίας εἰς ἄφεσιν ἁμαρτιῶν', in Zeit und Geschichte, ed. Dinkler (1964), p. 123.

[2] Structure et théologie de Luc I–II, pp. 111–16.

[3] Harald Sahlin, Der Messias und das Gottesvolk, Studien zur protolukanischen Theologie (1945), pp. 328 ff.

[4] Luke is able to reproduce such nationalistic statements, of course, because he equates the church with Israel (Conzelmann, The Theology of St Luke, p. 163).

The fact that this national-political motif is concentrated in the Magnificat and Benedictus has led Dibelius (Botschaft und Geschichte, 1, 14) and Winter ('Magnificat and Benedictus—Maccabean Hymns?', op. cit.) to conjecture that they were originally Jewish eschatological hymns which have been adapted by a Baptist (Winter) or a Christian (Dibelius) redactor. It should be noted, however, that the same nationalism is latent in the limitation of deliverance to Israel, an idea not confined to these two hymns. In any case, Christians felt no compunctions about employing these hymns and must be held responsible for their content.

hope has been spiritualized is unclear. In any case, Jesus is regarded as the Davidic messiah in the infancy narrative.

But it is not with the 'messiah of Israel' that the story of redemption in Luke 1 begins, but rather with John the Baptist. Did the sources then originally picture John as the 'messiah of Aaron'? For his priestly lineage is guaranteed through both parents. His father is of the course of Abijah, the eighth course of the sons of Zadok (I Chron. 24: 10). Of all the sons of Levi, only the sons of Zadok had preserved the sanctuary when Israel went astray (Ezek. 44: 15; 48: 11). Therefore they alone are allowed to minister before the Lord at his altar (Ezek. 40: 46). At this very altar one of the faithful (Luke 1: 6) sons of Zadok receives the revelation that *his* son will inaugurate the messianic *Heilzeit*. That son, John, will be like Elijah, the great prophet-priest of old, who had kindled the fire of God on a water-soaked sacrifice and restored true offerings to Israel (I Kings 18).[1] Even his mother performs a priestly function for her counterpart Mary by blessing her (1: 42, 45). But the strongest indication that a 'two-messiahs' view may lie behind Luke 1–2 is the manner in which the annunciation, conception, birth, rejoicing, circumcision, naming, greeting and growth of John are placed parallel to those of Jesus as if these men were co-redeemers, co-deliverers, the dual instruments of God's salvation.[2]

[1] Some circles expected Elijah to restore the manna, the sprinkling water, the anointing oil and perhaps even the rod of Aaron, all of which symbolize priestly functions (Mekilta on Exod. 16: 33; all rabbis concerned flourished from A.D. 80–120). Elijah was variously reported to be of the tribes of Gad, Benjamin or Levi. In those traditions in which his Levitical descent is stressed, Elijah is the High Priest of the messianic age, and is thus a colleague of the messiah rather than his forerunner (cf. Strack–Billerbeck, *Kommentar zum NT aus Talmud und Midrash*, IV, 791–8; T. W. Manson, *The Sayings of Jesus*, p. 69; and J. Jeremias, 'Elias', *TWNT*, II, 930–43). Jeremias suggests that the priestly messiah of the Test. XII Pat. is identified with Elijah due to the association of Mal. 3: 1; 4: 5 f. (Elijah as the angel of the covenant) with 2: 4–5 (the covenant of Levi).

Some have conjectured that the messiah of Aaron expected by Qumran was identified with Elijah, since Mal. 3: 1–4: 6 pictures Elijah as the restorer of true sacrifices to the temple (cf. A. S. van der Woude, 'Le Maître de Justice et les deux Messies', *La Secte de Qumran*, 1959, pp. 131–4). There is no evidence for this view, however, since Mal. 4: 5 f. does not seem to have been utilized at Qumran, nor is there a single clear reference to Elijah.

[2] Levi was born and blessed before Judah (Gen. 29: 34; 49: 5 ff.). In the Book of Jubilees 31: 4–20, Levi and Judah are blessed as the representatives

It has long been recognized that the prophecies concerning John in Luke 1: 14–17 and 76 f. are based on the prophecies dealing with the messenger of the covenant in the Book of Malachi. Laurentin, however, was the first to suggest the extent to which the identification is carried out and to see in it a reference to John's priestly messiahship.[1] The parallels are as follows:

Mal. 2: 4 Levi	Luke 1: 5 John is of the house of Levi
2: 6 'he turned many'	1: 16 'He will turn many'
2: 6 'He walked with me' (הָלַךְ אִתִּי)	1: 17 'He will go' (יֵלֵךְ)
3: 1 'to prepare the way *before me*' (לְפָנַי)	'*before Him*' (לְפָנָיו)
4: 5 f. 'I will send you *Elijah*' 'he will turn the heart of fathers to their children'	'in the spirit and power of *Elijah*' 'to turn the hearts of the fathers to the children
3: 18 'you shall distinguish between the *just* and the *wicked*'	and the disobedient to the wisdom of the *just*,
3: 1 'to prepare the way'	and to prepare for the Lord a people prepared'
4: 5 'Behold, I will send you Elijah the *prophet*'	1: 76 'And you, child, will be called the *prophet* of the Most
2: 6 'he walked' (הָלַךְ) 'before Me' (לְפָנַי)	High: for you will go (תֵּלֵךְ) before the Lord (לִפְנֵי יהוה) to prepare his ways'
2: 6 'True instruction was in his mouth'	1: 77 'to give knowledge of salvation'

The point of the 'midrash' is that John the Baptist fulfils the role of this prophesied messenger of the covenant. The prototype of this messenger is Levi (Mal. 2: 4–6), he is charged with enforcing the covenant of Levi (Mal. 2: 4, 8, 10), he will purify the sons of Levi and reprove the wicked priests (Mal. 1: 6; 2: 1), he will restore right offerings and sacrifices and cleanse the sanctuary desecrated by their wrongs (Mal. 3: 2 b). And like the prophet-priest Elijah he is charged with converting men before the Lord comes.

But if John is the messenger of the covenant who prepares the way of the Lord, then is Jesus 'the Lord' who 'will suddenly come to his temple' (Mal. 3: 1)?

of the priestly and kingly lines, respectively. Note that in Luke 1: 26 John (of Levi) is said to be six months older than Jesus (of Judah).

[1] Laurentin, *Structure et théologie*, pp. 56–60.

Mal. 3: 1 'The Lord'	Luke 1: 17, 76 Jesus is called 'the Lord' in a context where God would normally be inferred (also 1: 43; 2: 11)
will suddenly come to his temple	2: 22–38 Jesus is manifested in the Temple
4: 2 'But for you who fear my name the sun of righteousness shall rise'	1: 78b Jesus will be the 'day-spring' or 'dawn from on high' who will bring light and peace (1: 79)
3: 5 After the preparation the Lord himself 'will draw near to you for judgement'	2: 34 f. Jesus will cause the fall and rising of many, that the thoughts out of many hearts may be revealed
3: 3 When the Lord comes to the temple to purify it, 'he will sit as a refiner'[1]	2: 46 Jesus is found sitting in the Temple
'he will purify the sons of Levi'	2: 47 teaching the Teachers in the Temple
'till they *present right offerings* to the Lord'	2: 22 Jesus *himself* is '*presented*' to the Lord, along with a sacrifice which strictly follows the ordinances of the Law (2: 24)

In Christian circles 'the Lord' when used of Jesus is equivalent to 'the messiah', that is, the Davidic or kingly messiah. It is therefore conceivable that some Christian exegete has developed a midrash on the basis of the prophecies of Malachi, in which Jesus represents the messiah of Israel ('the Lord') and John the messiah of Aaron (the restorer of the covenant of Levi).

Subsequently, according to this theory, the 'two-messiahs' view was suppressed in the traditions underlying Luke 1–2, for the idea was implicitly 'heretical' from the point of view of the higher Christology which in time came to prevail. The suppression of the 'two-messiahs' theology would have been of a piece with the suppression of Ebionism generally.

It is possible that Luke 1–2 itself contains polemic against this 'two-messiahs' view. For instance, Jesus' Davidic ancestry is traced through Joseph (Luke 1: 27). But Mary is said to be the 'kinswoman' (συγγενίς—1: 36) of Elizabeth, thereby gaining

---

[1] Mal. 3: 1b–4 probably referred originally to the messenger, not to the Lord.

claim to priestly heritage. Some redactor may be seeking by this means to establish Jesus' solidarity with the sacerdotal tribe and to insinuate that Jesus, not John, is the priestly messiah.[1] Note also the number of priestly names in Jesus' 'Davidic' genealogy in Luke 3: 23–38.[2] Likewise only those elements of the Malachi tradition are retained which portray John as forerunner, and the parallelism of their nativities is continually slanted in favor of Jesus. John is not placed beside Jesus, but beneath him.[3]

To its credit we must say that this 'two-messiahs' theory at least takes seriously the priestly elements in the traditions about John. More important, it provides an explanation for the remarkable parallelism between the accounts of Jesus and John. Perhaps the ambiguity which led Kraeling to say that the forerunner concept of John is totally lacking in Luke 1–2[4] arises from the fact that this forerunner concept has been inadequately superimposed upon a dual-messiahship construction. Conceivably, this 'two-messiahs' concept might have been employed by

[1] Laurentin, *Structure et théologie*, p. 114; so also Milik, cited by Burrows, *More Light on the Dead Sea Scrolls*, p. 69. The dual-messiahship idea was also unsatisfactory Christologically because the priestly messiah was in certain matters given ascendency (Burrows, *ibid.* p. 310).

[2] There are two Levis, as well as other names associated with the priest-hood—Mattathias twice, one of them probably the father of the Maccabees, and his father Semein (= Simeon?—I Macc. 2: 1–5); Melchi (= Melchiah?—a priest in Neh. 10: 3; 12: 42, a Levite in Neh. 8: 4); Jesus (high priest in Hag. 1: 1, 12, 14; 2: 2, 4; Zech. 3: 1, 3, 6, 8, 9; 6: 11); Eliezer (a priest in Ezra 10: 18, 23); Judah (a priest in Neh. 12: 36, a Levite in Neh. 12: 8, Ezra 10: 23); Joseph (a priest in Neh. 12: 14); Eliakim (a priest in Neh. 12: 41). Even where these Old Testament persons do not fit the genealogy, they serve as evidence that these names were used by priestly families.

[3] The same 'oblique parallelism' obtains in the representation of their respective parents. The angel reprimands Zechariah when he acts incredulous, whereas Mary's identical response brings forth a revelation from God. And though Zechariah and Elizabeth are exemplary in their fidelity to the commandments of God, it is Mary who is singled out as the 'favored one' who has 'found favor with God' to bear his Son. Zechariah and Elizabeth are filled with the Holy Spirit and prophesy; but Mary conceives by the Holy Spirit. Mary goes to Elizabeth and receives her blessing, but Elizabeth is incredulous at the favor granted her, 'that the mother of my Lord should come to me' (1: 43; compare Matt. 3: 14!). And while the neighbors rejoice with Elizabeth at the birth of John, at Jesus' birth the angels of heaven praise God. Such 'Christological jealousy' by the church is the spawn of religious veneration, not anti-Baptist polemic.

[4] *John the Baptist*, p. 17.

John's former disciples in a tentative attempt to comprehend the relation of John to Jesus.

Laurentin's theory is, of course, highly conjectural. There is simply not enough evidence available, either in the infancy narrative or in the background literature, to consider the theory established. Several questions remain unanswered. For instance, to what extent are the priestly elements incidental? Do they represent historical or theological data? Is it not the case that, while John's priestly lineage is greatly emphasized, John himself is never depicted as a priest or as performing priestly functions, except in so far as these are identical with the functions of a prophet? Is not John's role confined to that of '*the* prophet of the Most High' (Luke 1: 76)—a conception of him which might have been equally at home in Baptist as well as Christian circles? And was there really a wing of the church which embraced the two-messiahs belief?

It may be that there is a simpler explanation for the parallelization of John and Jesus as co-redeemers:

The very first disciples of Jesus had in all probability been disciples, just before, of a man whom they had come firmly and surely to regard as the Prophet; and although they now had a new master, they were not ready to dispossess their old one of this role. (The Fourth Gospel does, but this is much later.) John the Baptist was and, so far as these first Christians were concerned, would continue to be the Prophet... To Jesus might be ascribed all the other traditional terms and offices, but that of the Prophet had been already occupied and preempted. It belonged, for them at least, irrevocably to John.[1]

In the church John's role as the eschatological Prophet would thus have been made secure by the earliest Christians, who had previously been and, in a real sense, still were John's disciples. The birth stories about the Prophet John and the Messiah Jesus could therefore be set side by side, since it was through these two acting in concert that God had redeemed his people. This would mean that there was no other conception of the relationship between John and Jesus than that which the infancy

---

[1] John Knox, 'The "Prophet" in the New Testament Christology', *Lux in Lumine*, p. 25. Cf. also H. H. Oliver, 'The Lukan Birth Stories and the Purpose of Luke–Acts', *NTS*, x, 2 (1964), 220 f., who believes that 'in Luke i–ii John is identified as the prophet, while Jesus is the Messiah of Israel and Aaron (i.e. the Teacher)'.

narrative already presents; that is to say, the forerunner/ messiah concept and the two-messiahs concept were *one*, with John the 'Prophet-Messiah' (and hence forerunner), and Jesus the Messiah of David (and Aaron?—Luke 1: 36; 2: 41–51).

In the final analysis it may not be possible to reach firm ground in deciding whether the church conceived of John as the 'Priest-Messiah' or as the 'Prophet-Messiah'. It is significant, however, that at every level of Luke 1–2 it is the *church's* traditions and conceptions which are before us, and not a 'Baptist Nativity' pirated from a group of John's disciples. The first two chapters of Luke are not chapters in the history of Christian polemic and apologetic. Quite the reverse, they are *the earliest Christian hagiology*, in which the birth of John is lavished with all the devotion due to the first Christian saint.

(3) *The Evangelist Luke and the Infancy Narrative*

How does the picture of John in Luke 1–2 compare with his representation in the rest of Luke's work? In spite of all that scholars have said to the contrary,[1] the conceptions are quite similar. In both sections of Luke's Gospel there is the same emphasis on John as prophet (1: 76*a*; 7: 26), forerunner (1: 76*b*; 7: 27; 3: 4), and teacher (1: 77*a*; 3: 10–14). He preaches a forgiveness (1: 77*b*; 3: 3) which will prepare men for salvation (1: 77*a*; 3: 6), and his birth as well as his preaching can be described as 'good news' (1: 19; 3: 18). The same elements are de-emphasized: his identity with Elijah (1: 17—he is merely endowed with the same spirit and power as Elijah; 3: 16—the description of his garments is omitted due to their association with Elijah); his message of judgement and doom (1: 16 f. only by implication; 3: 10–14); his role as baptizer (not referred to in chapters 1 and 2; compare 3: 21 f.).

Likewise the same view of redemptive history is operative in Luke 1–2 as in the rest of Luke–Acts. The coming of Jesus is not the end of history but rather the beginning of the middle epoch of history. The kingdom does not come with his coming, but rather the king. Consequently John does not usher in the kingdom but is the king's forerunner ('Lord'—1: 76*b*, 17). The prophecies of Luke 1–2 consistently look forward to the coming

[1] Cf. for instance Conzelmann, *The Theology of St Luke*, p. 172.

of this king (1: 32, 33, 69, 78; 2: 11, 26). What is most remarkable in all these prophecies is that nowhere is the restoration of the kingdom anticipated. This is especially striking in 2: 25, where the 'consolation of Israel' is not the restoration of the kingdom (though Luke knows this is the usual sense of the phrase, as Acts 1: 6 shows), but rather the birth of the Davidic king (2: 30). Again, when Mary rejoices that the Lord has 'put down the mighty from their thrones and exalted those of low degree' (1: 52), she looks forward to the 'enthronement' of Jesus as king (cf. 1: 33) but not to the conquest of the heathen. The Benedictus suggests political liberation (1: 71–5); it is all the more remarkable then that it says nothing of the restoration of the kingdom. Thus when Anna would console those who are 'looking for the redemption of Jerusalem', she speaks 'of *him*' (2: 38); furthermore the reader is probably expected to understand in the word 'Jerusalem' a reference to the elect, not the state.[1] This distinction between king (present) and kingdom (still future) should not surprise us; it is implicit in the very idea of the 'second coming' of Christ. Luke makes it even more consistent because he so keenly believes that this is the actual state of things: Jesus reigns as king until the restoration of all things at the end of time (Acts 3: 21; 1: 7 f.). This explains also why the theme of judgement and wrath is gradually dropped from John's message (cf. Acts 13: 24 f.; 10: 37; Luke 1–2), for *Jesus* will bring the Judgement when he returns (Luke 21: 34–6).

In another important way the picture of John in Luke 1–2 corresponds to that in the rest of Luke's works: John's relation to 'Christian time'. On the one hand John is included in the central period of salvation. His birth is proclaimed as 'good news' (1: 19). He is still, as in Mark 1: 1 ff., the 'beginning of the Gospel', so much so that his nativity is placed prior to that of Jesus. The events surrounding his birth signal the revival of prophecy (1: 67; 2: 25–35, 36–8), visions (1: 8–22, 26–38; 2: 8–15), and the effusion of the Holy Spirit (1: 15, 35, 41, 67; 2: 25, 26), all of which Luke regards as peculiarly characteristic of the Christian dispensation. Nor does the fact that John is the forerunner exclude him, for Luke considers this role as an aspect of

---

[1] The only reference to the kingdom in Luke 1–2 is in 1: 33*b*, but here βασιλεία should probably be translated 'kingship' or 'dominion' since it stands in synonymous parallelism with βασιλεύσει, 'reign', in 1: 33*a*.

the messianic time itself and integrally connected with salvation (1: 77).

Yet Luke 1–2 is, as a whole, an extended prophecy. Its joy is proleptic; it springs from anticipation, not actuality. Nowhere is it said that the birth of these children is the 'now' of salvation; their role is always future.[1] John is not 'born' the forerunner: he 'will be' the forerunner at the time of his manifestation to Israel (1: 15–17, 76 f., 80; 3: 2). Nor is Jesus born the 'Savior, who is Christ the Lord' (2: 11), for it is only at his baptism that 'he will be called the Son of the Most High' (1: 32–5; 2: 34 f.; 3: 21 f.). Luke 1–2 remains a *Vorgeschichte*; both Jesus and John are born, so to speak, in the old aeon. The anticipated benefit of their *ministries* is the cause of rejoicing, not the fact of their birth itself. What Plummer said of the Benedictus might thus be applied to the entire infancy narrative: it is 'the last prophecy of the Old Dispensation and the first of the New'.[2]

(4) *Conclusion*

We have found no reason to believe that the Lukan infancy narrative rests on a 'Baptist Nativity' or 'Gospel' which emanated from a competitive Baptist sect. The evidence suggests, on the contrary, that the church possessed these legends about John from the very beginning by virtue of the fact that it was itself an outgrowth of the Baptist movement. The traditions of John's birth developed from the outset in parallel with the birth stories of Jesus. Each reverent detail added to one tradition soon found its echo in the other. Together they evolved in an artful symmetry expressive of the conviction that through these two men God had wrought the redemption of Israel.

It is possible, though extremely conjectural, that the parallelism between the two narratives derives from a 'two-messiahs' theology in which John was the priestly and Jesus the Davidic

[1] In Luke 1: 68 Zechariah proclaims at the birth of his son that God *has* visited and redeemed his people, but the rest of the poem (*vv.* 76–9) makes it clear that these aorists are to be understood in a proleptic sense. (The aorists, of course, reflect the faith of the church.)

[2] *The Gospel According to St Luke* (1896), pp. 38 f. Cf. Conzelmann, *The Theology of St Luke*, p. 193 n. 5: '...the birth story does not introduce one of the three phases [of the central period of salvation], but forms a preliminary scene of manifestation for the whole of the Gospel.'

messiah. The materials for such a construction certainly lay at hand. By far the simplest hypothesis, however, is that John was regarded from the beginning, by both Baptists and Christians alike, as the eschatological prophet, and that this conception of him has been retained in the infancy narrative, the one alteration being that the Coming One whom John announced is identified as Jesus. Thus Baptist traditions could be absorbed without jeopardy to the position of Jesus, and Baptists could enter the church without renouncing John.

In any case, the infancy narrative in its final form grants Jesus complete priority, and Luke has brought the whole account into conformity with his conception of John as the forerunner of Christ and the inaugurator of the period of fulfilment.

C. POLEMIC AND APOLOGETIC IN LUKE–ACTS

It has been asserted by many writers that Luke is engaged in polemic against the followers of John the Baptist. Luke 3: 15 has often been cited as proof that John was being called messiah by his followers. The passage is somewhat indefinite:

As the people were in expectation, and all men *questioned* in their hearts concerning John, whether *perhaps* he were the Christ, John answered them all...

Luke apparently believes that this editorial comment reproduces the actual historical situation, and not without justification (cf. Mark 6: 14, 16; 8: 28); even Josephus leaves the distinct impression that such messianic thoughts in regard to John were not far from the people's mind.[1] Note, however, that no one overtly identifies John as the messiah. John's reply is intended to cut off such a line of thinking before it goes farther. There can be little question that Luke has *some* traditional authority for the statement that there was, if not a belief, at least the suggestion of a possibility, that John might be the messiah. What we need to know, and what Luke 3: 15 does not tell us, is whether Luke is directing John's denial against a *contemporary*

---

[1] *Antiq.* XVIII, 5, 2: '...and when everybody turned to John—for they were profoundly stirred by what he said—Herod feared that John's so extensive influence over the people might lead to an uprising (for the people seemed likely to do everything he might counsel)' (cf. Appendix, p. 116).

Baptist group, or whether he is simply recording what he regards to have been the actual situation in John's day.

The same inconclusive result obtains from an examination of 3: 18–22. By three changes Luke removes all subordination of Jesus to John: John is imprisoned before Jesus is baptized; Jesus baptizes himself;[1] and the Holy Spirit comes, not as a result of John's mediation, but because Jesus *prayed*. To what extent the motive behind these changes is simply Christological and to what extent it is polemical it is impossible to decide, unless Luke's views can be discovered elsewhere.[2]

And elsewhere Luke's attitude toward John is generally favorable. In 11: 1 (no par.; cf. also 5: 33) the disciples urge Jesus to follow the example of John and teach them to pray. Luke no doubt is familiar with John's practices (cf. 3: 10–14, and below, pp. 85 f.); but he would never have pictured Jesus as the imitator of John had he been polemically engaged with a group which claimed that John, and not Jesus, was the Messiah.[3]

Again, Luke traces the apostleship back to the 'baptism of John', thus rooting the church in the ministry of the Baptist (Acts 1: 22). He consistently uses the generalized hyperbole 'all' to describe the popular response to John (John preached '...to *all* the people of Israel', Acts 13: 24; also Lk. 3: 3, 21; 7: 29; 16: 16; 20: 6); this certainly manifests no desire to detract from his stature! And when Luke quotes the Q passage, 'among those born of women none is greater than John; yet he who is least in the kingdom of God is greater than he' (7: 28), he does so not in

---

[1] Βαπτισθέντος is intended as middle ('baptized himself') since no one else is there to baptize him.

[2] C. R. Bowen ('John the Baptist in the New Testament', *AJT*, xvi, 1912, 92), following Schleiermacher, believes that Luke 3: 1–20 derives from an independent Baptist source. So also Harald Sahlin, *Studien zum dritten Kapitel des Lukasevangeliums* (1949). These views overlook the fact that the Christian church was a direct outgrowth of the Baptist movement and possessed these traditions from the very beginning.

The deletion of the phrase ὀπίσω μου in 3: 16 might also reflect polemic, yet it could as likely indicate a Christological aversion to anything that would detract from the stature of Jesus—in this case the idea that Jesus was a disciple of the Baptist (cf. also p. 55 n. 2 above).

[3] Flender is correct in saying that the prayer requested by Jesus' disciples is something quite new, and not to be compared with the prayer of John's disciples (*St Luke*, p. 85). But this is not because John is 'the representative of the old world', but because in Luke's eyes he is subordinate to Jesus, as forerunner to Lord.

order to stress John's subordination but rather his greatness, as the verses which follow show: '(When they heard this all the people and the tax collectors justified God, having been baptized with the baptism of John...)' (7: 29). Luke has not even 'heard', 7: 28 *b*! Finally, the fact that John plays such a key role in *Heilsgeschichte* indicates that Luke has nothing to fear from Jesus' predecessor. We see only the same tendency as in Matthew, to fix limits on the evaluation of John which would safeguard the distinctiveness of Christ.

But what of Acts 19: 1–7? Here Paul discovers in Ephesus a group of twelve 'disciples' or 'believers', terms which, in the absolute sense used here, always designate Christians in Acts. Yet they have only received the baptism of John and have neither received the Holy Spirit nor recognized Jesus as 'the one who was to come after' John. Are these people Baptists, or are they 'half-Christians', mavericks who have lived out of contact with the developments of 'orthodox' Christianity as represented by Paul? The evidence for either view seems equally strong. The only proper approach, as Käsemann has shown,[1] is to ask what Luke intends by this pericope. And Luke obviously, by his designation of this band as 'disciples', regards them as incomplete or 'half-Christians'. Yet by so doing he creates a historical monstrosity: Christians who know nothing of the Holy Spirit or the Lordship of Jesus! Apparently the source originally told about the conversion of some Baptists to the Christian faith, and Luke has transformed the picture to serve his own purposes.

Had Luke intended to present the conversion of these disciples of John as an example for other Baptists to 'go and do likewise', he would certainly have left the tradition unchanged, for that apparently was its original intent. If Luke nevertheless ignores the apologetical/polemical possibilities of the passage, we can only conclude that the situation which gave it rise no longer exists, or is at least regarded by him as of little consequence.[2]

---

[1] Ernst Käsemann, 'The Disciples of John the Baptist in Ephesus', *Essays on New Testament Themes*, tr. by W. J. Montague (1964), pp. 136–48.

[2] That Luke is capable of biting polemic is shown by his treatment of Simon Magus in Acts 8: 9–24. The Clementine Homilies aver that Simon was a disciple of the Baptist and succeeded Dositheus as a leader of the Baptist movement (II, 18–32). He drifted into Christianity, and later founded

Instead, Luke redirects the passage to speak to the problem of apostolic authority as it touches upon the essential marks of a Christian: baptism and the conferring of the gift of the Holy Spirit. The passage is thus brought into line with Acts 8: 4 ff. and 10: 44 ff.[1]

As his tradition made John into the herald of Jesus, so Luke has gone on to make John's disciples into an odd species of Christian and thus he has radically eliminated any suggestion of real rivalry. Such a presentation can certainly only have been possible *if Luke knew of the existence of a Baptist community by hearsay alone* and was not obliged to attach to it any real significance because, for him at least, it belonged to a past already remote. Only in such circumstances as these could he dispense with concrete polemics and content himself with painting over the tradition.[2]

his own gnostic sect, centered in the erotic myth of Helena (cf. E. Stauffer, *Jerusalem und Rom im Zeitalter Jesu Christi*, 1957, pp. 101 f.). Luke apparently is speaking directly to Simonian Gnostics when he has Peter exclaim that Simon is 'in the gall of bitterness and in the bond of iniquity', and makes Simon entreat intercession from the apostles. It is all the more significant then that Luke does not connect Simon with Baptists even though, historically, Simonian gnosticism may have originated as a Samaritan wing of the Baptist movement (cf. B. W. Bacon, 'New and Old in Jesus' Relation to John', *JBL*, XLVIII, 1929, 49; Scobie, *John the Baptist*, pp. 163–77).

[1] Käsemann, 'The Disciples of John the Baptist in Ephesus', *Essays on New Testament Themes*, p. 142, submits that Luke has suppressed the clear reference to this Baptist group because 'the existence of a community owing allegiance to the Baptist could not be admitted without endangering gravely the Church's view of his function' as the forerunner of Jesus. By his editorial revisions Luke is deliberately 'portraying all disciples of John as standing to Christians in the relation of embryos' (*ibid.* p. 148). But the text as it stands suggests that Luke is unaware of the Baptist identity of this group altogether. He knows of no other John the Baptist than the one who bears witness to Jesus; hence the existence of a continuing Baptist group was for him incomprehensible (E. Schweizer, 'Die Bekehrung des Apollos, Ag. 18, 24–26', *Evangelische Theologie*, xv, 1955, 247 ff.).

[2] Käsemann, *op. cit.* pp. 142 f. (italics mine). E. Haenchen believes that Luke is seeking the conversion of Baptist disciples by means of Acts 19: 1–7, saying, in effect: John was simply the forerunner of Jesus, he lacked the really powerful (i.e. Spirit-bearing) baptism, therefore each one who belongs to John is nothing but an imperfect Christian. Those who understand this will therefore allow themselves to be 'properly' baptized 'into the Lord Jesus' (*Die Apostelgeschichte*, 1957, pp. 498 f.).

Conzelmann is closer to the truth, however, when he argues that, as far as Luke was concerned, after the death of John and his *heilsgeschichtlichen* super-

We may conclude, therefore, that while Luke is familiar with Baptist history and practice, he does not regard the disciples of John as contemporary rivals of the Christian church and is thus not directly engaged in polemic or apologetic with them. If the nativity stories of Luke 1–2 were originally composed by former Baptists with the conversion of other Baptists in mind, for Luke they no longer possess this function, but serve for him much as they do for Christians today, as an exercise in religious devotion. And while Acts 18: 24–19: 7 clearly indicates that the church had been encountering Baptist groups and converting (or seeking to convert) them, such engagements were no longer considered significant by Luke, who felt free to transform these traditions to serve the more serious contemporary problem of church order.

cession by Jesus, there no longer *was* a 'Baptist group'; therefore in characteristic fashion he turns these Baptist disciples into a special Christian group (*Die Apostelgeschichte*, 1963, pp. 109 ff.).

CHAPTER V

JOHN THE BAPTIST IN THE FOURTH GOSPEL

A. ANALYSIS OF THE TEXTS

(1) *The Prologue* (1: 1–18)

The presence of John the Baptist in the Prologue of the Fourth Gospel is astonishing. Nothing which the Evangelist says about John here could not have waited until 1: 19 ff.; indeed, several of the phrases in both sections are duplicatory.[1] If, as most scholars believe, *vv.* 6–8 and 15 are an intrusion into the poetic structure and flow of thought of the rest of the Prologue,[2] the question becomes acute: Why has the Baptist been so deliberately interjected into the Prologue?

There was a man sent from God, whose name was John. He came for testimony, to bear witness to the light, that all might believe through him. He was not the light, but came to bear witness to the light (1: 6–8).

John stands in utter distinction from the Logos-light to which he bears witness. The Logos is described in divine terms (θεὸς ἦν ὁ λόγος), John is simply 'a man' (ἄνθρωπος).[3] The Logos is πρὸς τὸν θεόν—'with' God (1: 1), at God's right hand; John is merely a delegated servant, sent παρὰ θεοῦ (1: 6). The Logos is the light (1: 4); John is but a witness to the light. One does not

---

[1] 1: 7 He came for testimony   1: 19 and this is the testimony
    1: 15 This was he of whom I   1: 30 This is he of whom I said,
      said, 'He who comes after   'After me comes a man who ranks
      me ranks before me, for he   before me, for he was before me'
      was before me'   1: 27 he who comes after me

[2] Cf. E. Käsemann, 'Aufbau und Anliegen des johanneischen Prologs', in *Libertas Christiana: Friedrich Delekat zum 65. Geburtstag*, ed. E. Wolf and W. Matthias (1957), pp. 75–99; E. Haenchen, 'Probleme des johanneischen "Prologs"', *ZThK*, LX (1963), 305–34; R. Schnackenburg, 'Logos-Hymnus und johanneischer Prolog', *BZ*, I (1957), 69–109.

[3] D. W. Baldensperger, *Der Prolog des vierten Evangeliums. Sein polemisch-apologetischer Zweck* (1898), p. 4.

believe *in* John but only *through* him (δι' αὐτοῦ, 1 : 7); but one believes in the Logos (εἰς τὸ ὄνομα αὐτοῦ—1 : 12). And, to complete the antithetical parallelism, the Logos 'was in the beginning' (ἦν ἐν ἀρχῇ, 1 : 2), but John 'came' (ἦλθεν, 1 : 7).[1]

The explicit denial in *v.* 8 that John 'was not the light' can be understood as simply a Christological safeguard to preserve the uniqueness of Jesus, or as a polemical rebuttal against a group of Baptists who were claiming that *John*, and not Jesus, was the 'light'. The polemical interpretation of *v.* 8 is supported by the qualification placed on 'light' in *v.* 9: Jesus is τὸ φῶς τὸ ἀληθινόν, the *true* light. False messiahs and self-styled emissaries of God were 'two-pence a dozen' in those days, to be sure; but it may be significant that the reference to Jesus as 'the true light' appears immediately after the denial that John was this light, and that the whole section 6–8 is bounded on either side by the strongest possible claims on this title for Jesus.

Verse 15 answers the vexed question of priority, with which each evangelist in succession has had to deal. The Fourth Evangelist is not content, however, to state merely that Jesus is *mightier* than John (Mark 1 : 7 par.). Instead he distinguishes John and Jesus qualitatively: 'He who comes after me ranks before (ἔμπροσθέν) me, for he was before (πρῶτός) me.' Jesus 'comes' after John, to be sure, but he 'was' before all things, for he is the Logos.[2] By this paradoxical transposition the Evangelist removes all threat of invidious comparison. Even if Jesus *appears* to be John's disciple (1 : 27; 3 : 22 ff.), the reader knows that he is prior (πρῶτός), ὁ λόγος, θεός, μονογενής, τὸ φῶς, and hence that he is of a different order entirely.

In *v.* 15 the Baptist witnesses, 'This was he of whom I *said*', but in *vv.* 6–8 John had said nothing. Yet in both passages we find the words μαρτυρίαν (7), μαρτυρήσῃ (7), μαρτυρήσῃ (8) and μαρτυρεῖ (15). What is important, therefore, is not what John says, but the fact that he is a 'witness' to Jesus' messiahship.[3] As

---

[1] Baldensperger, *Der Prolog des vierten Evangeliums*, pp. 6–9.

[2] *Ibid.* p. 44.

[3] *Ibid.* p. 41. The absence of a saying of John prior to *v.* 15 cannot be explained as the result of source conflation, since 1 : 6–8 and 15 both appear to be later additions to the Prologue by the Evangelist. Verses 6–8 and 15 are intrusions into the Prologue even if they are technically the original introduction to 1 : 19 ff. and the Prologue is the 'intruder', as R. T. Fortna argues ('The Gospel of Signs: A Reconstruction of the Chief Narrative Source

we shall see, the Evangelist's understanding of John's positive significance is totally comprehended in this term.

(2) *The Witness of the Baptist* (1: 19–51)

On the first day (1: 19–28) John alone appears, just as in Mark 1: 4–8 par. Yet only occasionally do we hear echoes of his preaching of repentance as it is recorded in the Synoptic Gospels.[1] The Evangelist has interpreted the figure of John completely under the perspective of his relationship to Christ as a *witness*. To this end he affixes a title to the section: αὕτη ἐστὶν ἡ μαρτυρία τοῦ Ἰωάννου. Every other role is sheared away. When the Jewish leaders inquire if perhaps he is the Christ, he demurs; in consternation they suggest lower titles: Elijah, prophet.[2] But the Baptist will have no title; he will be only the 'voice' of Isa. 40: 3. Not only does he reject the role of Christ, but he gives by way of denial a 'negative confession' that Jesus is the Christ; this is the point of 'he confessed, he did not deny, but confessed'. For confessing and denying Christ are strong themes throughout the Gospel (9: 22; 12: 42; 13: 38; 18: 25, 27).[3] This is underlined by the Baptist's denial, ἐγὼ οὐκ εἰμὶ ὁ Χριστός, for only Jesus can say ἐγὼ εἰμὶ.[4]

The Evangelist also sharply contradicts the earlier tradition that John was Elijah. For him the idea of a forerunner is anathema; notice how carefully he has already applied the antidote to it in 1: 1, 15. John is not the forerunner, for the Logos is already πρῶτός (1: 15, 30) and can have no forerunner. Since John is merely 'the voice', a witness to Jesus

Used by the Fourth Evangelist', unpublished doctoral dissertation, Union Theological Seminary, New York, 1965, pp. 193–7).

[1] Cf. C. H. Dodd, *Historical Tradition in the Fourth Gospel*, pp. 248–301.

[2] C. K. Barrett, *The Gospel According to St John* (1960), p. 145, notes that the question, 'Then why are you baptizing, if you are neither the Christ, nor Elijah, nor the prophet?', is no indication that these figures were expected to baptize. Rather it means, 'Why do you perform what appears to be an official act if you have no official status?' The question is equivalent to that in Mark 11: 27–33 par.

[3] *Ibid.* p. 144.

[4] E. Hoskyns, *The Fourth Gospel* (1947), p. 174. John 18: 6 shows that the Fourth Evangelist considers ἐγὼ εἰμὶ in at least some instances to be a divine name equivalent to that of God in Exod. 3: 14, for when Jesus utters these words his captors fall to the ground. Cf. also 4: 26; 6: 20; 8: 24, 58.

Christ, he no longer conforms to any known figure within the framework of Jewish expectation.[1]

In very much the same way as Matthew, the Fourth Evangelist aligns John with Jesus over against the hostility of 'the Jews' (1: 19). John is not one of 'the Jews', for this phrase is a technical designation for that portion of Israel which rejected Jesus.[2] A gulf is fixed between John and the Jews; he is a confessing Christian, they are the symbols of unbelief. The statement that the priests and Levites had been sent by the Pharisees casts grave doubt on the Evangelist's knowledge of Judaism prior to A.D. 70,[3] but at the same time this statement and the reference to 'the Jews' suggest that the chief opponents of the church in the Evangelist's day were Pharisees and not Baptists.

On the second day (1: 29–34) Jesus appears 'coming toward' John (1: 29, 35), yet he says nothing. The Evangelist's purpose is clear. With Jesus on the stage John can begin his positive witness to the Christ, pointing (as the artist Grünewald depicts it) to Jesus: 'Behold...*this* is he...and John bore witness [twice]...*this* is the Son of God...Behold.' If Jesus is the Lamb of God who takes away the sins of the world (1: 29, 36), then clearly John's baptism can no longer be for the forgiveness of sins. We see him baptize no one, nor is he once called 'the Baptist' in this Gospel. John's baptism is solely for the purpose of manifesting to the world its need for the purification which Christ alone brings (1: 31). Heavy emphasis therefore falls on the qualifying phrase 'I came baptizing *with water*' (1: 31, 33), for Jesus is 'he who baptizes with the Holy Spirit'. When the Evangelist says of Jesus that the Holy Spirit ἔμεινεν ἐπ' αὐτόν, he underlines the distinction between Jesus and the water purifiers (both John and the Jews—cf. 2: 6). *Jesus* has the Holy Spirit and will give it to his own. Over against all other religious communities into which one enters by water, stands the Christian church with water and the Spirit (3: 5).

Apparently Jesus has already been baptized before 1: 19 ff. begins (note the past tenses in 1: 30–4). The same Christological

[1] Barrett, *St John*, p. 144; cf. also Raymond E. Brown, 'John the Baptist in the Gospel of John', *New Testament Essays* (1965), pp. 138–40.

[2] Bultmann, *Das Evangelium des Johannes* (1957), p. 59.

[3] Barrett, *St John*, p. 145.

factors which had already caused Matthew and Luke to revise the baptism narrative have caused the Fourth Evangelist to omit the scene altogether. Jesus has no need of John's ministrations. Therefore the revelation at the baptism is directed, not to Jesus (as in Mark 1: 11), but to John, who twice confesses that, previously, 'I myself did not know him' (1: 31, 33). The Baptist is only a blind tool in God's hand, certainly not, as some might claim, the master and teacher of Jesus.[1]

On the third day (1: 35–42) Jesus again is walking, and John again bears witness. As a result several of John's disciples follow Jesus (1: 37). The language of discipleship adorns the section: 'rabbi', 'come', 'they followed Jesus', 'they stayed (ἔμειναν— cf. John 15: 1 ff.) with him'. It is *a priori* quite probable that a number of Jesus' first disciples were followers of John (cf. Acts 1: 22).[2] At the same time, however, these 'calling' stories can be seen to serve polemical-apologetical interests, if we may assume that the response of the first disciples is intended as an example to other Baptists to do likewise.[3] For the Evangelist has sum-

---

[1] Baldensperger, *Der Prolog des vierten Evangeliums*, pp. 72 f. Pierson Parker conjectures ('Bethany Beyond Jordan', *JBL*, LXXIV, 1955, 257–61) that the 'Bethany' where all these events take place is the same Bethany where Lazarus lived, two miles from Jerusalem (11: 18). John is not now baptizing, but is bearing witness to what he discovered when he baptized Jesus earlier. Parker paraphrases 1: 28 therefore as 'these things took place in Bethany, which is across from the point on the Jordan where John had been baptizing'. This would explain the ease with which the Jerusalem delegation comes to John (1: 19); the presence of a fig tree (1: 48, 50), an impossibility in the Jordan wastes; and the fact that Jesus has lodgings here large enough to entertain guests. Later Jesus lodges in Bethany again (12: 1). 1: 19 ff. is therefore an interlude in the baptizing ministry of John, when he leaves the Jordan region in order to make his witness to Jesus as the Christ. This would also explain why the place where John baptizes in Transjordan is not called Bethany in 3: 26 and 10: 40.

Parker's theory is attractive. However, the translation of πέραν is somewhat forced. We may be faced with nothing more than confusion in the Evangelist's understanding of Palestinian geography. The question must therefore be left open.

[2] Bornkamm, *Jesus of Nazareth*, p. 145; Cullmann, *Peter*, p. 23. Bultmann, *Das Evangelium des Johannes*, pp. 4 f., suggests that the Fourth Evangelist had come into the church by way of the Baptist movement. So also Cullmann, 'L'opposition contre le Temple de Jérusalem, motif commun de la théologie johannique et du monde ambiant', *NTS*, v (1958/9), 164; and J. Jeremias, *The Central Message of the New Testament* (1965), p. 81.

[3] Baldensperger, *Der Prolog des vierten Evangeliums*, p. 67.

moned as corroborating witnesses to the testimony of John several leading pillars of the church, some of whom at least were John's former disciples. The first confesses Jesus as 'Messiah', the second confesses him as the one 'of whom Moses in the law and also the prophets wrote' (i.e. the Prophet—Deut. 18: 15?), the third confesses him as 'the Son of God', 'the King of Israel'. Thus essentially every role explicitly denied John in 1: 19 ff. is applied to Jesus.[1]

On the fourth day John disappears. The call of the disciples continues. John 1: 51 rounds out the whole section by designating Jesus as the Son of man, the new Jacob-Israel. The break with Judaism is complete.

The wedding feast at Cana follows (2: 1–11), 'on the third day'. Since the third day has already passed, we must conclude that the third day after the last-mentioned day is meant, that is, the seventh day since the events narrated began.[2] The sequence of days scheme shows that the Cana episode is intended as a part of the foregoing events. The real end of chapter 1 is thus 2: 12.[3] The miracle is not to be taken at face value. It is a sign (2: 11), 'the first of his signs', which resulted in the manifestation of his glory and caused his disciples (who to this point only provisionally believed—'they stayed with him *that* day', 1: 39) to

[1] Dodd, *The Interpretation of the Fourth Gospel*, p. 293. The only title not transferred to Jesus is that of Elijah. This is in line with the author's rejection of apocalyptic generally and his rejection of the forerunner motif in particular. It is possible that 3: 13 is an attack on the assumptions of Enoch, Moses and Elijah: 'No one has ascended into heaven but he who descended from heaven, the Son of man.' That the Evangelist is familiar with the tradition that John is Elijah is seen in 3: 28, where 'sent before him' echoes Mal. 3: 1. Cf. also 1: 6, 31 (compare *Dial. cum Trypho* 8); 5: 35 (compare Sirach 48: 1); 1: 8—'he was not the light' (compare Midrash on Ps. 43: 1 [134*a*]: '"Thy light" [Ps. 43: 3], that is, the prophet Elijah' [cited by Jeremias, *TWNT*, II, 935 n. 75]).

[2] Pierson Parker, 'Bethany Beyond Jordan', *JBL*, LXXIV (1955), 260 f.; T. Barrosse, CSC, 'The Seven Days of the New Creation in St John's Gospel', *Catholic Biblical Quarterly*, XXI (1959), 514. Barrosse suggests that the seven days scheme of 1: 19–2: 12 symbolizes the seven days of the new creation with Cana concluding the 'week' and representing the establishment of Jesus' church, the 'new creation' (cf. 2: 1, 11, 12). W. D. Davies has suggested to me that the six jars for the Jewish rite of purification represent the six week-days of Jewish history preceding the messianic sabbath banquet on the seventh day.

[3] Dibelius, *Johannes der Täufer*, p. 112.

believe in him. Two clues are given. 'On the third day' is admittedly an awkward way of designating the seventh day. In Christian parlance, however, the phrase suggests the passion and resurrection of Jesus. This allusion to the passion is underscored by 2: 4, where Jesus says 'my hour has not yet come', for Jesus' 'hour' in the Fourth Gospel consistently refers to his death (cf. 7: 30; 8: 20; 12: 23, 27; 13: 1; 17: 1, etc.).[1] The miracle is therefore a sign of what will be accomplished by the death of Christ. The second clue is the six stone jars of water 'for the Jewish rites of purification' (2: 6). The meaning is apparently that the water of Judaism is replaced by the wine of Christianity, the wine being symbolic of the blood of Christ.[2] And since in 1: 31, 33 water is designated as *the* element of John's baptism, the transformation of the water may also signify the transformation of the Baptist movement. For John's former disciples become believers as a result of this 'sign'.[3]

Nevertheless it is difficult to restrict the polemical thrust of the Cana episode to Baptists alone; it strikes at Judaism in its entirety.

(3) *The Second Witness of John* (3: 22–4: 3)

This section is rife with contradictions. John 3: 1–21 ostensibly took place in Jerusalem, yet in 3: 22 Jesus goes to Judea! He baptizes in Judea (3: 22), yet apparently ends up at Aenon near Salim in Samaria ('here he is', 3: 26).[4] He baptizes, yet he does not baptize (3: 26; 4: 2), everyone receives him, no one receives him (3: 26, 32)! And John continues to baptize, even though the

[1] Barrosse, *art. cit.* p. 514.

[2] Dodd, *The Interpretation of the Fourth Gospel*, pp. 297 ff.

[3] Dibelius, *Johannes der Täufer*, p. 112.

[4] A. M. Hunter, 'Recent Trends in Johannine Studies', *ET*, LXXI, 6 (1960), 164–7, declares that 'the location of Aenon may now be regarded as reasonably certain'. It lies near the headwaters of Wadi Far'ah in Samaria. So also Scobie, *John the Baptist* (1964), pp. 163 ff. Barrett, *St John*, p. 183, remains skeptical. Bacon cites evidence that there was a strong Samaritan gnostic wing of the Baptist movement and that John 3: 23 ff. represents the struggle between Christians and Baptists there toward the close of the first century. Samaria is the traditional resting place of John ('New and Old in Jesus' Relation to John', *JBL*, XLVIII, 1929, 52 ff.). Cf. also Kraeling, *John the Baptist*, p. 194 n. 9. Goguel suggests that this passage originally emanated from a Baptist group, since it is John, not Jesus, who is so precisely located in 3: 23 (*Life of Jesus*, pp. 272–5).

sole point of his baptism, the manifestation of Jesus to Israel (1: 31), is already accomplished. Various theories of source redaction or transposition have been advanced in order to explain these contradictions.[1] We are concerned, however, only with the Evangelist's understanding of the narrative.

Why are Jesus and John placed side by side as rival practitioners of the same rite? It is, of course, quite possible that Jesus actually practiced baptism as a disciple of John for a period before his public ministry began.[2] But the Evangelist is making an entirely different point: Jesus has his own disciples and baptizes independently of John, without a sign of subordination and with greater success! The Evangelist thus contradicts the Synoptic report that Jesus began his public ministry only after the imprisonment of John. Jesus' work does not just follow the Baptist's but parallels it. Jesus is not simply John's successor. By placing them momentarily side by side the Evangelist shows how the full sunshine has hidden the glow of the moon: 'Here he is, baptizing,' says the Evangelist, 'and all are going to him' (3: 26);[3] and again, 'Jesus was making and baptizing more disciples than John'. Of all this John heartily approves, for now his 'joy is full'. In fact he can scarcely efface himself enough: 'he must increase, but I must decrease.' And, as if the Evangelist is still insecure in John's denial of the messianic titles (1: 20; cf. 1: 8), he has him humble himself once more: 'I am not the Christ.' Even John's disciples are called to bear witness to his denial (3: 28).

Already we have seen that the author is loath to rest with a merely quantitative comparison between Jesus and John, and chapter three is no exception. Jesus is not just a better baptizer, he is the Bridegroom (3: 29). John is his friend and ally, but the distinction is absolute. Jesus alone comes from above, John is of the earth (3: 31).[4]

[1] M. Goguel, *Jean-Baptiste*, pp. 86 ff.; cf. also Bultmann, *Das Evangelium des Johannes*, pp. 122 ff., who transposes 3: 22–30 after 3: 36 and attaches 3: 31–6 to the Nicodemus discourse (3: 1–21).

[2] Goguel, *Life of Jesus*, p. 315.

[3] Dibelius, *Johannes der Täufer*, pp. 109–11. In the Synoptics '*all*' went out to *John*; now this '*all*' emphasizes the superior response received by Jesus.

[4] It is possible that the phrase ἐκ τῆς γῆς reflects the saying of Q (Luke 7: 28), 'among those *born of women* none is greater than John', and is a retort to the Baptist claim that John is therefore greater than Jesus.

This distinction between John and Jesus is brought out in the controversy over purification between John's disciples and a Jew (3: 25).[1] The dispute appropriately takes place on a non-Christian level. Jesus withdraws from the whole argument (4: 1) and from baptism itself since something greater than water is coming, baptism in the Spirit, which he will provide after his death. The Spirit alone will make the water of baptism efficacious.

Therefore Jesus allows his disciples to baptize under his authority (4: 2), even though this baptism is provisional and incomplete. For the question of purification is, at the moment, irrelevant, since the purpose of baptism is to manifest Jesus to Israel (1: 31). 'If anyone should inquire', wrote Chrysostom, '"In what was the baptism of the disciples better than that of John?" we will reply: "In nothing"': both were alike without the gift of the Spirit, both parties had one reason for baptizing, and that was to lead the baptized to Christ.'[2] Thus John wisely turns the dispute into an opportunity to witness to the Christ and to correct his own disciples. *Jesus* is the bridegroom, the Lamb of God, and Jesus alone, not baptism, takes away the sins of the world. Only through the death of Jesus are water and Spirit united (3: 5), for out of his pierced side flow both water and blood (19: 34 f.), united by the Spirit in the water of baptism and the wine of the Eucharist (cf. I John 5: 6–8).[3]

'He must increase, but I must decrease' (3: 30). This is John's swansong, his last word in the gospel. It is also the formula under which every statement about John stands.[4] His witness abides (5: 32–6; 10: 40–2), but John slips off the stage. His death is not even mentioned, so unimportant is his person.

---

[1] Goguel believes that 3: 25 originally read 'Jesus' instead of 'a Jew' in the Evangelist's source (*Jean-Baptiste*, pp. 86 ff., following Bentley and Sember, Kreyênbuhl, Baldensperger and O. Holtzmann).

[2] 'Homily XXIX on John 3: 22', in *Nicene and Post Nicene Fathers*, XIV, 100; text in *PG*, series 2, LIX, 167. Cf. also Tertullian, *De Baptismo*, in *Corpus Christianorum*, Series Latina, I, 284 ff.

[3] Schweitzer, *The Mysticism of Paul the Apostle*, tr. from the German ed. of 1931 by W. Montgomery (1956), p. 355.

[4] T. F. Glasson ('John the Baptist in the Fourth Gospel', *ET*, LXVII, 1955–6, 245 f.) notes that the sections treating John the Baptist become progressively shorter, and regards this as conscious artistry based on the model, 'he must increase, but I must decrease' (3: 30). It is more likely, however, that this sequence is simply the side effect of a progressive decrease of interest in the Baptist as the narrative moves along.

(4) *The Value of John's Witness* (5: 31–47)

The Evangelist has until now been assembling the testimony of witness after witness: John (1: 7 f., 15, 32, 34; 3: 26), the voice of the Father (1: 33), the first disciples (1: 41–50), the Scriptures (2: 17, 22), the Samaritan woman (4: 29, 42), even the church (3: 11—'we'). Now he sorts these witnesses out according to their various merits.

Jesus waives claim to testify on his own behalf (5: 31), though, as we learn in 8: 14, this self-witness is valid in his particular case. The witness of John is adduced only as an *argumentum ad hominem* to those who set store by the Baptist's work and teaching (5: 33–5).[1] But Jesus does not rely on such human, secondary testimony as John's when he has greater testimony than this: his own works and the voice of the Father. In addition to these witnesses Jesus mentions still another, one which the Jews should readily understand but do not: the Scripture (5: 39). The position of ἡ γραφή is analogous to that of John: like the Baptist, the Scripture is not the Light but rather bears witness to the Light. Like John, it points not to itself but to its fulfilment in Christ (cf. also 8: 56; 12: 41). But both are secondary witnesses because they only testify to the revelation and are not the revelation itself. Only Jesus, the Word made flesh, makes God known (1: 18).[2] Implied here is the Evangelist's hermeneutical principle that Jesus Christ is the locus of God's revelation in all ages. The corollary of this principle, therefore, is that there is a specifically Christian exegesis, resulting from the incarnation, which sees the whole Scripture as a witness to Jesus Christ.[3] By regarding their biblical studies as ends in themselves the Jews have perverted the real function of the Scripture and have brought condemnation upon themselves, for the Scripture directs men away from itself to Jesus, exactly as did John the

[1] Dodd, *The Interpretation of the Fourth Gospel*, p. 329. But this appears to have been, not merely his own circle of disciples, but a large portion of the general population (cf. Mark 11: 32, etc.; Jos. *Ant.* XVIII, 5, 2).

[2] J. Louis Martyn, 'The Salvation-History Perspective in the Fourth Gospel', unpublished doctoral dissertation, Yale University, 1957 (used by permission of the author), pp. 319 f. 'ὁ λόγος σάρξ ἐγένετο means that ἡ γραφή ceases to be the sole locus of God's self-revelation and becomes one μαρτυρία among several' (*ibid.* p. 81).

[3] *Ibid.* pp. 320 f.

Baptist.[1] Likewise the Jews rejoiced for a while in John's light but failed to heed his witness (5: 35).[2]

'The Jews' again are the focus of indictment in this section, for those who 'were willing to rejoice for a while in his light' (5: 35) are not John's disciples (or the church) but those same Jewish officials ('the Jews'—5: 10, 15, 16, 18) who had 'sent to John' in 1: 19 ff. (5: 33a). Their accuser is therefore Moses, not John the Baptist (5: 45). Here again, the primary polemical thrust is directed against Pharisaical Judaism and not the Baptist community.

(5) *John's Witness Was True* (10: 40–2)

Whatever the historical value of this brief notice, the Fourth Evangelist uses it to state for a last time the relationship of Jesus to John. Jesus flees to the place across the Jordan where John at first baptized,[3] thereby affirming once more his solidarity with John. And as always, John's significance is fenced about by a negative judgement before his positive value is acknowledged:

'John did no sign, but everything that John said about this man was true.' And many believed in him there.

In John's own bailiwick people testify that he did no sign and that Jesus is superior.[4] It is difficult to decide whether those who

---

[1] It is inaccurate to say, as does Barrett, that John the Baptist represents the Old Testament (*St John*, p. 140; also pp. 142, 144; cf. also Jean Steinmann, *John the Baptist and the Desert Tradition*, 1958, p. 174—'He plays in Christianity the same role as the Old Testament, which he sums up in his person...'). For both the Baptist and the Scriptures are independent, secondary confirmations that Jesus is the Christ; they are not dissolved into each other by virtue of their comparable functions. Note how they are held apart in 5: 31–47.

[2] Dodd hears in the phrase 'a burning and shining lamp' (5: 35) an echo of the description of Elijah in Sirach 48: 1—'Then the prophet Elijah arose like a fire, and his word burned like a torch' (*Historical Tradition*, p. 266).

[3] For historical theories, see Goguel, *Life of Jesus*, p. 406.

[4] E. C. Colwell, *John Defends the Gospel*, pp. 32–8. In the peculiar usage of the Fourth Gospel John could do no sign, since 'signs' are by definition miracles by which Christ reveals his glory. Bultmann believes that the denial that John did signs indicates a need to counter reports of miracles by the Baptist, and cites Mark 6: 14 as evidence (*History of the Synoptic Tradition*, p. 302 n. 1). But Raymond E. Brown argues concerning Mark 6: 14 that

believe in Jesus across the Jordan are John's former disciples, or others who 'came to' Jesus from elsewhere.[1] Yet why would the author have the people say that 'John did no sign' unless there were those who were affirming that he had?

B. POLEMIC AND APOLOGETIC IN THE
FOURTH GOSPEL

We now return to our earlier question: why was mention of John the Baptist interpolated into the Prologue? Baldensperger long ago suggested that a Baptist sect had fastened upon the Christian estimation of John and had developed it into a rival 'christology', with John as the 'light' of men. As a means of combatting this false estimation of John the Fourth Evangelist has set out a systematic correction of both the Baptist christology and those Synoptic traditions which were open to such misuse.[2] There is strong evidence for this view, as we have already seen: the denial that John is the light (1: 8); John's violent refusal of the Christological titles (1: 19 ff.); the contrast between baptism in water (John) and in Holy Spirit (Jesus) in 1: 31, 33; 3: 22 ff.; the implication in 3: 31 that John is 'out of the earth' whereas Jesus alone is above all things because he is 'from above'; John's denial that he is prior (1: 15, 30); the assertion that Jesus baptized more than John; John's confession of Jesus' superiority (3: 22–4: 2); the statement that John's witness is merely that of a human and is unnecessary (5: 34, 36); and the comment that John did no sign (10: 41). Furthermore, there do appear to be allusions to a Baptist movement in the Gospel. For instance, John pointedly says to his disciples in 3: 28, 'You yourselves bear me witness, that I said, I am not the Christ'. And the fact

'the implication there is probably not that miracles were associated with John the Baptist, but that one who had come back to life would have marvelous powers' (*The Gospel According to John*, 1966, 1, 413). This is no doubt true of Mark 6: 14, but it does not preclude the possibility that John's disciples were ascribing miracles to him by the time John 10: 40–2 was written.

[1] There is no archaeological evidence that a Baptist community was located in Perea.

[2] *Der Prolog des vierten Evangeliums. Sein polemisch-apologetischer Zweck* (1898). This thesis was first suggested by J. D. Michaelis, *Einleitung in die göttlichen Schriften des Neuen Bundes* (1788), p. 1140.

that John's disciples leave him to follow Jesus may be intended as an example for other Baptists to do likewise.[1]

An additional confirmation of the theory of polemic is the argument from the structure of the Gospel.[2] Of the seven sections which refer to the Baptist in the Fourth Gospel, five are accompanied by a break in the sense or by textual dislocation, or they lie at points of juncture between two sources. The two exceptions are 1: 19–36 and 5: 32–6, both of which are integral to the context and are obviously related, 5: 33 referring back to the sending of the deputation in 1: 19. The other references to John appear to be editorial. This is virtually indisputable in the Prologue (1: 6–8 and 15).[3] It is almost as clear in 3: 22–30, which, besides its own internal difficulties, interrupts the discourse of Jesus and creates the impression that 3: 31–6 is spoken by the Baptist. 4: 1–3 is probably redactional, for the purpose of getting Jesus to Galilee via Samaria. Likewise 10: 40–2 is an editorial *tour de force* to remove Jesus from the environs of Jerusalem for the Lazarus narrative which follows.

Without quibbling over the complexities of source analysis in the Fourth Gospel, it does seem clear that for contemporary reasons additional references to John the Baptist have been intruded, whose historicity appears, on the whole, groundless, for the purpose of stressing the inferiority of John the Baptist to Jesus and of defining his relationship to the Christian faith.

Is there external confirmation for the continued existence of a Baptist sect which revered John as messiah? The scant references

[1] It is possible that the First Epistle of John reflects this same polemic when it asserts (5: 6), 'This is he who came by water and blood, Jesus Christ, *not with the water only* but with the water and the blood' (C. R. Bowen, 'John the Baptist and the New Testament', in *Studies in the New Testament*, ed. R. J. Hutcheon, 1936, p. 75).

[2] See the controversial statistical analysis by A. Q. Morton and G. H. C. MacGregor, *The Structure of the Fourth Gospel* (1961), pp. 61–3, which in this regard at least appears to be correct.

[3] C. R. Bowen, 'Prolegomena to a New Study of John the Baptist', in *Studies in the New Testament* (1936), p. 31, comments that the Baptist 'makes havoc of the carefully constructed literary Prologue, especially at the point where he intrudes into the super-historical realm, when as yet he has not appeared in time (verse 6). As Wellhausen remarks, he "carelessly drops into eternity"...Modern students note how enormously simplified the Prologue would be if the Baptist could be deleted...'

to 'Hemerobaptists' in the early fathers are of no help,[1] since we know neither the beliefs of the sect nor its relationship to John or his disciples. Likewise most scholars are of the opinion that the references to John the Baptist in the Mandaean literature are late, and that neither John nor his disciples are in any way connected with the rise of the Mandaean cult.[2]

The Pseudo-Clementine literature, however, does witness to a belief in John as messiah similar to that suggested by the Fourth Gospel:

Recognitions I, 54:

Yea, some even of the disciples of John, who seemed to be great ones, have separated themselves from the people, and proclaimed their own master as Christ.

[1] Justin, *Dial. cum Trypho*, 80 ('Baptists'); Eusebius, *Eccles. Hist.* IV, 22, 7 ('Hemerobaptists'); Epiphanius, *Panarion*, XVII ('Hemerobaptists') and XIX ('Osseans'); *Apostolic Constitutions*, VI, 6, 5 ('Hemerobaptists'). J. Thomas, *Le Mouvement Baptiste en Palestine et Syrie* (1935), p. 36, denies any connection between the Hemerobaptists and John or his movement. The reference to John as a Hemerobaptist in Ps.-Clem. Hom. II, 23 is a polemical anachronism directed at a related but independent group. On this point cf. also Charles H. H. Scobie, *John the Baptist*, p. 193.

[2] John the Baptist never appears in any Mandaean liturgical, magical or baptismal text. References to him are, without exception, quite late, often in Arabic (*Jahja*). He reveals no mysteries or teaching, is never pictured as a messiah or savior or founder of the sect, and does not even institute the rite of baptism (Hibil-Zīwā does). Repeated references to the 'Jordan' are nowhere associated with John, nor is Mandaean baptism an initiatory repentance-rite. All of the John-material rests on the Gospels, especially Luke, and on extra-canonical Christian and Islamic legends. Concludes Kurt Rudolph, '*John the Baptist and his disciples had, according to the finds of our investigation of the sources, no relation to the Mandaeans*', though both groups probably had a common ancestor in the sectarian baptist movements of the Jordan region (*Die Mandäer*, 1961, I, 80, italics his; cf. also I, 65–80; II, 382 n. 1, and 348–57). So also J. Thomas, *Le Mouvement Baptiste* (1935), pp. 260 ff.; C. H. Dodd, *The Interpretation of the Fourth Gospel*, pp. 115–30; E. S. Drower, *The Mandaeans of Iraq and Iran* (1962), pp. 2 ff. Thomas (following Brandt), Drower and Dodd believe that John rose to prominence in Mandaean thought during the period of Islamic conquest when religious toleration was contingent upon possession of sacred books and the veneration of a prophet. Consequently the Mandaeans seized upon John, who already possessed a place of honor in the Koran, and simultaneously committed much of their tradition to writing.

Rudolph agrees that references to John are consistently late, but places them earlier than Islamic times, John being an 'eponymous hero' imported to justify Mandaean lustrations in contrast to Christian (and Jewish?) rites.

Recognitions I, 60:

And, behold, one of the disciples of John asserted that John was the Christ, and not Jesus, inasmuch as Jesus Himself declared that John was greater than all men and all prophets. 'If then', said he, 'he be greater than all, he must be held to be greater than Moses, and than Jesus himself. But if he be the greatest of all, then must he be the Christ.'[1]

Elsewhere in the Pseudo-Clementines John ('Elijah') is paired opposite Jesus in a series of 'syzygiai', in league with such characters as Cain, Esau, Aaron, Simon Magus and the Antichrist (Hom. II, 17; cf. Recog. III, 61). In Hom. III, 22 John is referred to as one 'born of woman' and therefore of the feminine (fallen) order, whereas Jesus, as the Son of man, is masculine (heavenly) —a familiar gnostic motif. Finally, we find in Hom. II, 23–4 (Recog. II, 8) a very late legend connecting John with the rise of the gnostics Dositheus and Simon Magus. These hostile passages, of uncertain date and provenance, witness at least to the belief of their transmitters that the disciples of John had constituted one of four Jewish sects opposed to the church (Sadducees, Samaritans, Scribes and Pharisees, and Baptists). J. Thomas thinks that the polemic against John in the Clementines attests to the continued existence of a baptist sect in the contemporary environment.[2] In any case the Clementines preserve the memory that John had been hailed as Christ by some of his 'followers', whatever their actual relationship to him.[3] This

---

[1] *Ante-Nicene Fathers*, VIII, 92 f. (For a critical edition cf. B. Rehm, *Die Pseudoklementinen II Recognitionen*, *GCS* (1965), LI, 39, 42 f. For references to the Homilies, see same author and series, *I Homilien* (1953), vol. 42.) Ephraem of Syria has a parallel version based possibly on a common source (see J. Thomas, *Le Mouvement Baptiste*, pp. 116 ff., where the text is reproduced).

[2] *Le Mouvement Baptiste*, pp. 122 f.

[3] Cullmann believes (*The Christology of the New Testament*, p. 26) that the Baptist sect witnessed to by the Pseudo-Clementines understood 'messiah' to mean the same as 'eschatological prophet' and so regarded John as the Prophet-Messiah. John Knox has recently developed this suggestion in a most provocative way ('The "Prophet" in the New Testament Christology', *Lux in Lumine*). If John was regarded as the prophet-messiah by his followers then the titles 'Christ', 'Elijah' and 'the prophet' (John 1: 20 f.) would be identical in Baptist parlance, and the rejection of these titles for John by the Evangelist would be an explicit rejection of the Baptist Christology. Dodd fails to take this into account (*Historical Tradition*, pp. 265 f.).

creates a strong presumption in favor of Baldensperger's thesis of polemic.[1]

This polemical theory cannot be accepted without certain qualifications, however. It is methodologically illegitimate, for instance, to reconstruct the views of John's disciples by reversing every denial and restriction placed on John in the Fourth Gospel, as Bultmann and Bauer have done. By their line of reasoning, John was worshipped as Elijah, prophet, messiah, the Light and the Life of men, a wonderworker, the pre-existent Logos through whom all things were made, indeed, even as the Word made flesh![2]

If such an advanced 'John-cult' had in fact antedated the Fourth Gospel, John would never have been conferred such an exalted role by the Evangelist. On the contrary, we would have expected to have seen John pictured as a false messiah, the anti-christ, or as 'one who comes in his own name' (5: 43), or to have been accorded the same animosity which we find later in the Pseudo-Clementines. In developing his representation, all the Evangelist needed to know was that there were those who con-

[1] Thomas, *Le Mouvement Baptiste*, pp. 132 ff., also finds anti-Johannite polemic in Marcionite writings (Epiphanius, *Panarion*, XXVI, 6–7; XLII, 11), but without justification (text in K. Holl, *GCS*, XXV, 282–4 and XXXI, 127, respectively).

According to Marcion John proclaimed a Jewish messiah conversant with the Old Testament creator-God and had not expected a messiah like Jesus at all. John therefore belonged to the old dispensation (Tertullian, *Adv. Marcionem*, IV, 18, in *Corpus Christianorum*, Series Latina, I, 588 ff.). What we have here is not polemic against Baptists, but rather examples of Marcionite exegesis which project gnostic teachings upon the New Testament.

Nor are there traces of polemic against John's disciples in the newly discovered Gospel of Thomas. Its information about John is drawn wholly from New Testament traditions. In Saying 47 John is portrayed as the 'psychic' man as opposed to the true Gnostic (Matt. 11: 11), and in Saying 53 he may represent the last Old Testament prophet. But there is no attack against John or allusion to his movement. Saying 78 (Matt. 11: 7–8) no longer even applies to him. (Cf. R. M. Grant with D. N. Freedman, *The Secret Sayings of Jesus*, 1960, *loc. cit.*)

[2] Bultmann, *Das Evangelium des Johannes*, pp. 4 f., 29 ff., 57 ff., 300 n. 4; Walter Bauer, *Das Johannesevangelium* (1925), pp. 13–16. Bultmann also suggests that the Prologue of the Fourth Gospel was originally a Baptist hymn to John. Arguments such as these are defective in at least three ways: (1) they fail to allow for the possibility of any advance in the argument by the Fourth Evangelist, whose retorts are probably more direct and clear than the original assertions and anticipate further lines of attack; (2) they vastly

tinued to follow John and who applied to him messianic ascriptions.[1]

For the fact is that the Evangelist does not treat the Baptist in the same manner that he treats 'the Jews'. His polemic against the latter is open and unqualified. But nowhere does he regard John as an enemy, nor does he attack his sect or even censure it for its unbelief. And here in the Fourth Gospel, more than anywhere else, the church is regarded as a direct outgrowth of the Baptist movement (1: 35 ff.; 3: 22 ff.; 10: 40 ff.). The only issue at stake is Christological, and it is possible to explain many of the Christological distinctions between John and Jesus by means other than recourse to the theory of polemic with a Baptist movement.[2] Some of the Evangelist's 'polemical' references

exaggerate the importance of the Baptist movement and the amount of anti-Baptist polemic in the New Testament; and (3) their approach is not sufficiently comprehensive in that they fail to take into account the theological, typological and devotional use of the John-traditions by the church.

At the other extreme, C. H. Dodd (*The Interpretation of the Fourth Gospel, passim,* and *Historical Tradition in the Fourth Gospel,* pp. 298 ff.) and C. K. Barrett (*The Gospel According to St John, passim*) refuse to acknowledge the presence of any direct anti-Baptist polemic whatever.

[1] It is not even necessary to suppose that John was regarded as 'the Light' (John 1: 8) by his followers. If the Prologue was a Christian hymn already in popular use, as appears most likely, and John the Baptist has been intruded into it, then the language of the interpolations (*vv.* 6–8, 15) would have been dictated by the immediate context and by the leading ideas of the Evangelist.

[2] Cf. for instance the Severian baptismal liturgy, where Jesus is made to sanctify John's water for baptism; or the statement by Ephraem of Syria that Jesus grasps John's hand and places it upon his own head (cf. Baldensperger, *Der Prolog des vierten Evangeliums,* pp. 71 f.); or the *Gospel According to the Hebrews,* where the sinless Jesus is made to remark that he is unaware of any need for baptism by John (Jerome, *Dial. c. Pelagianos,* III, 2, in Hennecke–Schneemelcher, *New Testament Apocrypha,* I, tr. by R. McL. Wilson, 1963, pp. 146 f.); or the *Gospel of the Ebionites,* where John *falls down* before Jesus and entreats baptism (Epiphanius, *Haer.* XXX. 13, 7 f., in Hennecke–Schneemelcher, I, 157 f.); or the *Life of John According to Serapion,* where Jesus comforts John at Elizabeth's death by saying, 'Do not be afraid, O John. I am Jesus Christ, your master' (*ibid.* I, 407, 414–17); or the *Pistis Sophia,* c. 7 (*ibid.* I, 402 f.). In each case cited the issue is not polemic with Baptists but rather the attempt to circumvent statements in the Gospels which contradict the higher Christology of a later time.

By the same token, traditions which exalt John need not be ascribed to a Baptist community, for John's figure possessed sufficient mystique to attract considerable legendary development within the church. Cf. for instance St Augustine's sermons on John's miraculous conception and birth ('In

were already in process of development in the Synoptic Gospels, and we have found that these statements in the Synoptics reflect, on the whole, not polemic, but rather the need to place Christological safeguards on John's exalted role. The problem of Jesus' subordination to John, both as disciple and at baptism, had already brought forth a variety of solutions. The Fourth Evangelist's is perhaps the simplest and safest: Jesus is baptized *before* the narrative begins, and his baptism is for *John*'s sake, so that John might recognize the Lamb of God. Again, the Synoptic Gospels had, each in turn, struggled against the implication that Jesus, by following John, was inferior to him. The Fourth Evangelist handles this problem by recourse to Jesus' preexistence. And when he reduces John to a mere witness to Jesus, the Evangelist is merely completing the line of development which was already well on its way in Mark 1: 1–8. Nor does the call of the disciples necessarily serve a polemical purpose, not only because the account may well preserve historical truth, but also because Mark too had followed the account of the baptism with the call of four disciples. Likewise the one clear allusion to John's movement ('You yourselves bear me witness, that I said, I am not the Christ'—3: 28) is also, in essence, historical, since everything we know about John indicates that he did not, in fact, regard himself as the Christ.

The evidence for Baldensperger's thesis is, in short, somewhat ambiguous. Polemic and apologetic directed at contemporary 'disciples of John' clearly seems to be present, yet Baptists are not the chief opponents of the Evangelist's church. The prime target is Pharisaical Judaism, with the Baptist community deployed to one side, and somewhat closer to the church than to the emergent 'normative Judaism' of the Jamnian scholars.[1]

Natali S. Joannis Baptistae'—Sermons CCLXXXVII–CCXCIII, in *PL*, vols. 38–39), or Elizabeth's miraculous escape with John in *The Book of James (Protevangelium)*, XXII, 3 (Hennecke–Schneemelcher, I, 387), or the physical ascension of John's father Zechariah into heaven in *The Apocalypse of Paul* 51 (M. R. James, *The Apocryphal New Testament*, 1924, p. 554), or the 'Martyre, c'est-à-dire la naissance et la décapitation de Saint Jean le précurseur et le baptiste', ed. by F. Nau, *Patrologia Orientalis*, Tome IV, Fasc. 5 (1908), 521–41.

[1] Dodd's conclusion deserves careful consideration: 'The Baptist therefore is not treated as a rival who must be subpoenaed to give evidence in favour of Christ. He is claimed as one of Christ's own people. The *Sitz im Leben* which we should infer is one in which it was desired that persons who had followed the Baptist should be regarded as adoptive members of the

This is not surprising, since in the eyes of the Pharisees both Baptists and Christians belonged to the heretical sectarian baptist movement, and both paid allegiance to John. Apparently the Fourth Evangelist is still in dialogue with these Baptists, countering their hyper-elevation of John and wooing them to the Christian faith.

C. THE ROLE OF JOHN THE BAPTIST IN THE FOURTH GOSPEL

Yet, when due allowance for polemic and apologetic is made, one still has the distinct impression that only a part of the story has been told. For this polemic and apologetic is, after all, quite subtly expressed (by no means do all commentators even concede its existence!). It is for the Evangelist a subsidiary concern, served almost automatically by his primary purpose. For whether John is subordinated for reasons of polemic or for the sake of a higher Christology, or for both, this subordination is itself subordinated to the Evangelist's desire to portray John as *the ideal witness to Christ*, a theme to which he returns again and again. John is made the normative image of the Christian preacher, apostle and missionary, the perfect prototype of the true evangelist, whose one goal is self-effacement before Christ: 'He must increase, but I must decrease' (3: 30).[1] John is sent (ἀπεσταλμένος) from God (1: 6; 3: 28); he is an 'apostle' in a non-technical sense.[2] His whole function is to 'witness', that others might believe through him (1: 7, 8, 19, 20, 29–34; 3: 26, 28; 5: 33 f.).

Church...If the passage in Acts [18: 24–19: 7] has any significance as a pointer to what happened to the surviving followers of the Baptist, it suggests, not that they perpetuated a community carrying on a vigorous mission in rivalry with the Church, but that (so far as they did not remain within the Jewish fold) they were absorbed into the Christian Church; and this is in all probability the truth' (*Historical Tradition*, pp. 299 f.).

[1] This use of John by the Fourth Evangelist as a *type* of the true Christian witness and missionary is analogous to John's appropriation by the Mandaeans as the type of the true baptizer, and their designation of the 'Jordan' as any body of water in which true baptism can take place.

[2] The Fourth Gospel does not develop the technical idea of apostleship, ἀπόστολος appearing only once (13: 16). The verb is preferred, and is synonymous with πέμπω (Barrett, *St John*, p. 473). The emphasis falls therefore not on the office but on the missionary function of the one who is sent. The word has evangelistic rather than ecclesiastical connotations.

The Evangelist has thus projected upon John his own all-consuming purpose: 'that you may believe that Jesus is the Christ, the Son of God' (20: 31; cf. 1: 7, 29, 34, 36). Perhaps this explains the repeated use of the present tense in 1: 15: 'John *witnesses* (μαρτυρεῖ) concerning him and cries (κέκραγεν)[1] saying (λέγων)...'; likewise the words ἀπεσταλμένος εἰμὶ in 3: 28 form a timeless present: 'I am sent before him', sent perpetually, wherever the gospel is preached.

The Evangelist's portrait of John is thus intended more for the church than for Baptist circles. Far from being an enemy, John is Jesus' 'best man' (3: 29). In the same absolute sense as in Mark, John is still the 'beginning of the Gospel' (John 1: 6–8, 19 ff.). He stands with Jesus as a witness against 'the Jews' (1: 19 ff.; 5: 32 ff.), his witness is equivalent in value to that of the Old Testament (5: 33 ff.), and he assumes the role of the first confessing Christian (1: 29 ff.). John's 'Christianization' is now, in this Gospel, made complete. The 'baptizer' has become 'the friend', the forerunner has become 'the voice', the prophet has become a saint.[2]

The determining motive in the Evangelist's use of John is the desire to placard before the eyes of the church the ideal relationship of evangelist to Lord. With the same self-effacing disregard for title, for recognition and for a following, the Christian reader is summoned to identify with John and become transparent, invisible as it were, a 'voice' only, bearing witness to the Son of God.

This explains how it is that the Evangelist can annihilate the claims made for John without depreciating the man, and it illuminates the paradoxical relationship between debasing and exalting John throughout the Gospel. For John only embodies the same process of self-denial that all Christians are called to embrace, a self-denial which paradoxically leads to the most exalted of tasks: proclaiming Christ to the world.

[1] The perfect is used here with the force of a present (Barrett, *St John*, p. 140, citing Moulton, *Grammar of New Testament Greek*, I, 147; so also E. Haenchen, 'Probleme des Johanneischen "Prologs"', *ZThK*, LX, 1963, 333 f.).

[2] Dibelius, *Johannes der Täufer*, p. 143; Dodd, *Historical Tradition*, pp. 297, 299.

CHAPTER VI

CONCLUSION

We return now to the question with which we began our study: why is John the Baptist granted such an important role in the Gospel tradition?[1] The answer has customarily been that John was pressed into the service of polemic and apologetic against the sect of his disciples, the church seeking thereby to correct and convert its opponents out of the mouth of John himself. The results of our study indicate that, while an element of polemic and apologetic is present, it plays a secondary role and is, of itself, incapable of explaining the Evangelists' preoccupation with John.

We are now in a position to reconstruct the history of the relationship between the church and John's disciples, in so far as such reconstruction is possible. It is evident from the outset that John did not dream of founding a sect, but of preparing by baptism, *across* sectarian and party lines, a people prepared for the baptism of the Coming One (Matt. 3 : 11 f. par.). The inner circle of adherents who ministered to his needs and assisted in his work had their own style of life, to be sure, including fasting, sobriety, fixed forms of prayer, and ethical norms conversant with a repentant life (Mark 1 : 6; Matt. 11 : 16–18; Mark 2 : 18; Luke 11 : 1; Luke 3 : 7–14). But the vast majority of those baptized by John returned to their regular occupations to await the expected One (cf. Luke 3 : 8, 10–14). To one or the other of these circles Jesus and most (or all?—Acts 1 : 22) of his first disciples belonged.[2]

In the early period of the church, John's disciples continued to be regarded fraternally since both groups fully endorsed the ministry of John. For the most part the Baptist movement was absorbed into the Christian church (cf. Acts 19 : 1–7; John 2 : 1–11; Mark 1 : 16–20; John 1 : 37, etc.). The remaining holdouts first protested that the messiah had not come; then in defensive

---

[1] John the Baptist is named ninety times in the New Testament, exceeded in frequency only by Jesus, Paul and Peter.

[2] On these points cf. esp. C. Kraeling, *John the Baptist*, pp. 161–3 and *passim*.

reaction some proclaimed John messiah, apparently meaning thereby the eschatological prophet.[1] Using Christian sayings against Christians, they asserted John's superiority over Jesus by means of Jesus' own words, principally Matt. 11: 11a/Luke 7: 28a.

In response, the church hedged about its traditions concerning John with various defense-mechanisms whose purpose was not only to safeguard belief in Jesus as the Christ, but *to preserve John for the church.* On the whole, though, John's position in Christian theology was already secure by virtue of the continuing veneration of those in the church who had come to Jesus by way of John, and because the tradition itself was so uncompromising and unanimous in its declaration that the actual events proclaimed as 'gospel' by the church had begun with John.

And what of the subsequent history of the disciples of John? In order to answer this question we must place John the Baptist and his movement within the context of the 'baptist movement' generally, as a phenomenon of the Jordan River cleft.[2] These syncretistic Jewish sects, though fiercely independent, shared one thing in common: the centrality of baths or baptisms in lieu of sacrifice. As a broad movement of protest against contemporary piety, these groups were heterodox, schismatic, highly individualistic, quick to shift to the latest 'revelation', and capable of borrowing from one another without establishing relationships of dependency.

The apogee of the baptist movement was in the years 150 B.C.– A.D. 150, when Essenes, Nasoreans, Ebionites, Baptists, Elkasites and other sects, sub-sects, and even solitaries (e.g. Banus) flourished.[3] As these baptizing sects continued to spawn and

---

[1] John Knox, 'The "Prophet" in the New Testament Christology', *Lux in Lumine.*

[2] Following J. Thomas, *Le Mouvement Baptiste en Palestine et Syrie* (150 av. J.-C.—300 ap. J.-C.), 1935. I refer to the broad phenomenon of baptizing sects as 'the baptist movement' and to John's own disciples by the proper name 'Baptists' or 'Baptist movement'.

[3] J. Thomas, *Le Mouvement Baptiste*, p. 430. Thomas says earlier (p. 130): 'Instead of representing it [Ebionism] as just one heresy, we mean hereafter a conglomerate of communities diversely influenced and evolved...; we will speak of Ebionism*s* rather than of Ebionism.' Likewise 'Essene' is coming to be understood today less as a *species* than a *genus*, consisting of a manifold of groups variously constituted—not 'Essenism' but 'Essenisms' (cf. for instance M. Black, *The Scrolls and Christian Origins*, 1961, pp. 3–9). One might

proliferate, their significance waned proportionately. They receive passing notice by several church fathers, but soon were engulfed and absorbed by pagan gnosticism with its magic, astrology and polytheism, and finally dropped from sight altogether.

John was apparently made an eponymous hero by more than one branch of the baptist family. We have already seen how he was so used by the Mandaeans (above, p. 100 n. 2). We should not need reminding that he serves as a founding hero for the Christian church as well. Apparently the 'Hemerobaptists', of uncertain lineage, had claimed John, as had the Simonian Gnostics (Ps.-Clem. Hom. II, 23–4; Rec. II, 8). The persistence of John's popularity is attested to by Josephus, who, writing close to the end of the first century, still remembers that 'some of the people' blamed Herod's defeat by Aretas IV on his unjust execution of John (*Antiq.* XVIII, 5, 2). Not a party man, John's appeal transcended sectarian loyalties.[1] Each sect could therefore lay claim to him without subscribing to the unique features of his doctrine and practice or joining common cause with his surviving disciples.

John's memory and influence long outlasted that faithful circle which continued to await the One whose coming he preached. The groups with which the church engaged in polemic and apologetic toward the end of the first century in all likelihood possessed only the slenderest connection with John, neither perpetuating his work nor counting seriously as competitors with missionary Christianity.

Once the existence of a Baptist community is conceded, it becomes *a priori* likely that it produced and propagated traditions about John. Conjectures about the use of Baptist documents in our Gospels, however, have generally rested on a basic misconception of the relationship of the early church to the baptist movement, and to John's movement in particular. By anachronistically projecting back into its origin the later conflict between Christians and John's disciples, many scholars

---

compare the sectarian baptist movement with the contemporary Pentecostal movement in America, with its proliferation of countless groups united by a single 'rite' ('baptism of the Holy Spirit').

[1] Note the respect Josephus accords John in the reference cited above. There is no possibility of Christian interpolation in the passage (cf. Kraeling, *John the Baptist*, pp. 85 ff.).

have made the fundamental error of regarding the groups as separate and alien, whereas in actual fact *the church stood at the center of John's movement from the very beginning and became its one truly great survivor and heir.* The church thus already possessed a full store of authentic traditions about John from its very inception, and continued to be the primary locus for their legendary and theological elaboration. As Baptists continued to convert to the church, they no doubt brought with them oral traditions with which to supplement the church's treasury of lore about John. Some of these traditions may have eventually made their way into the New Testament. We have found no evidence in the Gospels, however, that written documents or 'Gospels' about John existed or were employed by the Evangelists.

As far as polemic and apologetic against 'Johannites' is concerned, we have already seen that it is explicit only in the Fourth Gospel. Traces of apologetic are clearly present in the sources employed by Luke, but appear to be directed primarily at converting the remnant of John's disciples and not against a rival messianic sect. Acts 19: 1–7 reveals that Luke possessed no concrete conception of the Baptist community,[1] and Luke 3: 10–14 and 11: 1, far from suggesting conflict, indicate that Luke was rather attracted by the historical image of John. Two passages in Q reveal the church hard at work to counter Baptist objections to the messiahship of Jesus (Matt. 11: 2–6, 11 par.), but neither Matthew nor Luke takes up the struggle. And in Mark no sign of antagonism with a Baptist sect is in sight. The theory of polemic and apologetic does not explain John's presence in the Gospels; it supplies but a piece of the puzzle.

It is rather John's role as 'the beginning of the gospel' which accounts for his positive religious significance for the writers of the New Testament. Under this formula each successive Evangelist has developed his own peculiar understanding of John's role. Thus Mark portrays John as Elijah incognito whose sufferings prepare the way of the Lord and serve as an example to the persecuted Christians at Rome. Matthew uses John as an ally of Jesus against the hostile front of opposition he was encountering in the Judaism of his day. The Lukan infancy narrative may reflect two views, an earlier conception of John

---

[1] Käsemann, 'The Disciples of John the Baptist in Ephesus', *Essays on New Testament Themes*, p. 143.

as the priestly messiah, in parallelism with Jesus the Davidic messiah, and a later view of John as the prophetic forerunner of Christ; or perhaps, as appears more probable, one view only, that of John as the eschatological prophet and Jesus as the messiah of Israel (and Aaron?). In any case, Luke accepts the traditional picture of John as the forerunner with minor changes and adapts it to his panoramic conception of *Heilsgeschichte*. And finally, the Fourth Evangelist holds up before the church the representation of John as a 'type' of the ideal Christian evangelist, whose function it is to witness that Jesus is the Christ.

Behind this diversity lies an unexpected unity: John the Baptist is 'the beginning of the gospel of Jesus Christ'. What is the source of this consistent basis for each successive portrait, and whence its persistence and authority? How do we account for the idea that the gospel begins with the ministry of John? A purely historical explanation is inadequate, for even though John *was* 'there' in the beginning, and baptized Jesus and many of his disciples, it is fairly certain that the sphere of John's activity was tangent to that of Jesus only at the point of baptism, and that John never confessed Jesus to be the messiah. Furthermore, the Gospels themselves preclude a purely historical solution since they are concerned with John primarily from a theological point of view.[1]

Since the source of the veneration of John seems to be the sayings of Jesus concerning him, especially those judged to be authentic in Q, we might presume that it was on Jesus' authority that John entered the gospel. But of itself this explanation is also inadequate, for the church was not therefore under any compulsion to develop the significance of John further, as it has done. Apparently the image of John as formulated by Jesus possessed an inner dynamic which accounts for its subsequent development.

This dynamic appears to have been Jesus' own view of God's saving activity and of John's role in it. The complaint of the Pharisees that John and Jesus have opened the kingdom to the

---

[1] It is significant that even the one non-Christian account of John, that of Josephus, treats John from a theological point of view. Josephus mentions John only by way of explaining that the defeat of Herod by Aretas IV was a divine judgement upon Herod for his execution of John.

lawless, immoral rabble is transformed by Jesus into a sweeping analysis of Israel's history: 'from the days of John the Baptist until now the kingdom of heaven has suffered violence, and men of violence take it by force. For all the prophets and the law prophesied until John' (Matt. 11: 12 f.). This passage shows that Jesus regards history as divided into at least two successive periods of divine activity: that of the Law and prophets which has now ended, and that which began with John and continues into the time in which Jesus is speaking, in which the kingdom is in some sense already present. Likewise his declarations of solidarity with John (Matt. 11: 7–11*a*, 16–19; 21: 32; Mark 11: 27–33) are, in essence, statements about the eschatological crisis which both sense to be at hand. Käsemann writes concerning Matt. 11: 12 f.:

…in it the Old Testament epoch of salvation history concludes with the Baptist, who himself already belongs to the new epoch and is not to be counted among the prophets. The situation in this epoch is that the kingdom of God has already dawned, but is still being obstructed. The Baptist has introduced it, and thus ushered in the turning-point of the aeons. Yet even he still stands in the shadow of him who now speaks and utters his 'until today'. Who but Jesus himself can look back in this way over the completed Old Testament epoch of salvation, not degrading the Baptist to the position of a mere forerunner as the whole Christian community and the whole New Testament were to do, but drawing him to his side and—an enormity to later Christian ears—presenting him as the initiator of the new aeon? But who then is this, who thus does justice to the Baptist and yet claims for himself a mission higher than that entrusted to John? Evidently, he who brings with his Gospel the kingdom itself…[1]

What is the source of Jesus' view that John 'stands at the dividing line between the period of anticipation and the period

[1] 'The Problem of the Historical Jesus', *Essays on New Testament Themes* (1965), pp. 42 f. So also James M. Robinson, *A New Quest of the Historical Jesus*, pp. 116 ff. Cf. Robinson's altercation with Bultmann, p. 117 n. 1, and his confirmatory citations in n. 2, where he quotes Dibelius, Lohmeyer and Kraeling in unanimous support for the view that 'the Baptist movement was taken by Jesus as the sign that God's kingdom was in fact drawing near' (Dibelius' phrase, *Jesus*, pp. 56 f.). So also E. Percy, *Die Botschaft Jesu*, pp. 198 ff.; W. G. Kümmel, *Promise and Fulfilment*, pp. 121 ff.; E. Fuchs, 'The Quest of the Historical Jesus', *Studies of the Historical Jesus*, tr. by A. Scobie (1964), p. 23.

in which the kingdom is present but in conflict'?[1] The Gospels all point to his baptism as the moment when Jesus was granted his initial insight into the meaning of the eschatological crisis proclaimed by John. Whether this was in fact the case we shall never know.[2]

Our investigation into the historical origin of the early Christian view of John has led us to the eschatological views of Jesus himself. *The conviction that John is 'the beginning of the gospel of Jesus Christ', and all of the Christian elaborations of it, are but the theological expression of a historical fact, that through John's mediation Jesus perceived the nearness of the kingdom and his own relation to its coming.* As each evangelist has developed this tradition in the light of urgent contemporary needs, he has done so in faithfulness to Jesus' basic conception, treating John, in a manifold of ways, as the one through whom the eschatological event centered in Jesus Christ is proclaimed to be 'at hand' to those for whom it continues to appear indefinitely remote.[3]

Nor did the church let the matter rest there. For since John prepares the way for Christ, *John could be used typologically by the church as a means of setting forth its conception of its own role in 'preparing the way of the Lord'.* And from this point it is only a short step to expressing through John the very essence of the Christian's witness (The Fourth Gospel) and of Christian existence itself (John's role in Mark). That is, the image of John personifies the frontier character of the Christian proclamation

---

[1] Kraeling's phrase, *John the Baptist*, pp. 156 f.

[2] Dibelius argues that only Jesus could have reported the baptismal event and its meaning for him, but had he done so surely a logion would have been recorded; since there is no logion the account is therefore unauthentic (*From Tradition to Gospel*, 1934, p. 274). Where then does the church learn that Jesus' ministry was triggered by this event if, on Dibelius' terms, the event is unknown and unknowable? Surely the church has not created the baptism of Jesus, with his resulting subordination to John. Cf. Kraeling's attempted reconstruction, *John the Baptist*, pp. 154 f.; Robinson's existentializing reconstruction is less persuasive (*A New Quest of the Historical Jesus*, p. 108). In the final analysis, however, the meaning of Jesus' baptism for him remains inaccessible to historical research.

[3] There is a certain irony in the fact that redaction-criticism should direct us to conclusions regarding the historical Jesus, since redaction-criticism was itself born, to a great extent, of skepticism over the possibility of a quest for the historical Jesus.

as it encounters men at the border of the times and calls them to receive the kingdom. For this reason it was absolutely essential that the church circumscribe John's role by means of various Christological safeguards, and protect his image against both external attack (Baptist and Jewish polemic) and internal distortion (by over-zealous homage rendered him by John's former disciples in the church, on the one hand, or by the outright rejection of John by the Jewish-Christian authors of the Pseudo-Clementines on the other). It was this carefully circumscribed typological use of John as the embodiment of the church's life in witness which became normative, not only for the Gospel accounts, but also for the hagiographical legends of the early centuries and for works of art and biographies of John right down to the present.[1]

Far from assigning to him a temporal and now accomplished task, it [the church] recognized him to be the one who will be for ever preparing the way for Christ and who, so to speak, stands guard at the frontier of the aeons. The way to Christ and into the kingdom of God did not merely at one time—in a moment of past history—lead through John the Baptist, but it leads once and for all only along that path of repentance shown by him. Faith in Jesus Christ is only there where the believer, for himself and within himself, lets the shift of the aeons take place in his own life.[2]

Why then did the church tamper with its traditions about John? Why, if it was being faithful to Jesus' basic conception, was it not merely content to 'rejoice for a while' in John's light without modifying the sources it had received?

Apparently the church acted as it did because it was interested, not in preserving a record of its origins, but in recreating in its own contemporary existence that crisis of decision with which John had shaken all Israel. Only by refracting its traditions through the spectrum of contemporary events was

---

[1] Cf. the masterpieces of Grünewald, El Greco and Rodin, each of which in its own way portrays John as a self-effacing witness to Christ; or the biographical tract, *John the Baptist, Missionary of Christ* (1953), by André Rétif, an impassioned plea, by an associate of the Cercle St Jean-Baptiste, for Catholic missionaries to be, like John, 'the dawn of salvation, the constant and disinterested friend of the Bridegroom, the very unassuming servant of the Word of God' (p. 120).

[2] Bornkamm, *Jesus of Nazareth*, p. 51.

the church able to reveal to successive generations its perception of John's actual impact on his own day and of the ongoing relevance of his work. If in bending the light the church has progressively discovered colors not originally visible, it has not thereby falsified or perverted the truth. To state the paradox as sharply as possible, the church preserved continuity with the past 'by shattering the received terminology, the received imagery, the received theology—in short, by shattering the tradition'.[1] It was not enough that one know who John was, but that one encounter, through the medium of his history, that same summons to judgement and repentance which he issued.

Therefore the Christian community, just for the sake of preserving intact the actual historical significance of John as they had experienced it, refused to allow the memory of John to slip uninterpreted into the past. Instead they were faithful to do what Jesus had already done: they kept John on the frontier of the aeons as the pioneer of the kingdom of God. The church did not preserve John as an historical fossil, but incorporated him in the *kerygma* itself, making him thereby a part of the continuing Christian proclamation. Consequently John the Baptist was, from the very first, and, through the faithful mediation of the New Testament Evangelists, continues to be, 'the beginning of the gospel of Jesus Christ'.

[1] Käsemann, 'The Problem of the Historical Jesus', *Essays on New Testament Themes*, p. 20.

THE ACCOUNT OF JOHN
IN JOSEPHUS

The passage is found in *The Antiquities of the Jews*, XVIII, 5, 2 = §§ 116–19 (translated by H. St John Thackeray in the Loeb Classical Library edition):

...but some of the Jews believed that Herod's army was destroyed by God, God punishing him very justly for John called the Baptist, whom Herod had put to death. For John was a pious man, and he was bidding the Jews who practiced virtue and exercised righteousness toward each other and piety toward God, to come together for baptism. For thus, it seemed to him, would baptismal ablution be acceptable, if it were used not to beg off from sins committed, but for the purification of the body when the soul had previously been cleansed by righteous conduct. And when everybody turned to John —for they were profoundly stirred by what he said—Herod feared that John's so extensive influence over the people might lead to an uprising (for the people seemed likely to do everything he might counsel). He thought it much better, under the circumstances, to get John out of the way in advance, before any insurrection might develop, than for himself to get into trouble and be sorry not to have acted, once an insurrection had begun. So because of Herod's suspicion, John was sent as a prisoner to Machaerus, the fortress already mentioned, and there put to death. But the Jews believed that the destruction which overtook the army came as a punishment for Herod, God wishing to do him harm.

SUPPLEMENTARY BIBLIOGRAPHY

A complete bibliography of works relevant to a study of John the Baptist would be prohibitive. Those already listed in footnotes are not repeated here; the Index of Names may be consulted to locate works already cited. Standard commentaries have also been omitted.

Albright, W. F. 'Recent Discoveries in Palestine and the Gospel of St John', in *The Background of the New Testament and Its Eschatology*, ed. by W. D. Davies and D. Daube (1956), pp. 153–71.

Bacon, B. W. 'The "Coming One" of John the Baptist', *The Expositor*, VI (1904), 1–18.

—— 'The Q Section on John the Baptist and the Shemoneh Esreh', *JBL*, XLV (1926), 23–56.

Bammel, E. 'Is Luke 16, 16–18 of Baptist Provenience?', *HTR*, LI, 2 (1958), 101–6.

Barnard, L. W. 'Matt. III. 11/Luke III. 16', *JTS*, VIII (1957), 107.

Barrett, C. K. 'The Lamb of God', *NTS*, I, 3 (1955), 210–18.

—— *Luke the Historian in Recent Study* (1961).

Barth, Karl. *Vier Bibelstunden* (1935).

Beasley-Murray, G. R. 'The Two Messiahs in the Testaments of the Twelve Patriarchs', *JTS*, XLVIII (1947), 1–12.

Benoit, P. 'Qumrân et le Nouveau Testament', *NTS*, VII (1961), 276–96.

Bergeaud, Jean. *St John the Baptist*, tr. by Jane W. Saul (1962).

Best, Ernest. 'Spirit-Baptism', *Novum Testamentum*, IV (1960), 236–43.

Betz, O. 'Die Proselytentaufe der Qumransekte und die Taufe im Neuen Testament', *RQ*, I (1958), 213–34.

Bieder, Werner. 'Um den Ursprung der christlichen Taufe im NT', *Theologische Zeitschrift*, IX (1953), 161–73.

Blakiston, Allan. *John the Baptist and His Relation to Jesus* (1912).

Boismard, M.-E. *Le Prologue de Saint Jean* (1953).

—— *Du Baptême à Cana* (1956).

Bonnard, Pierre. 'La signification du désert selon le Nouveau Testament...', *Hommage et reconnaissance: Karl Barth* (1946), pp. 9–18.

Botha, F. J. 'ἐβάπτισα in Mark i. 8', *ET*, LXIV (1953), 286.

Braun, H. 'Entscheidende Motive in den Berichten über die Taufe Jesu von Markus bis Justin', *ZThK*, L (1953), 39–43.

—— 'Qumran und das Neue Testament. Ein Bericht über 10 Jahre

Forschung (1950–1959)', *Theologische Rundschau*, Neue Folge, xxviii (1962), 97–234; xxix (1963), 142–76 and 189–261.

Braun, H. '"Umkehr" in spätjüdische-häretischer und in fruhchristlicher Sicht', *ZThK*, L (1953), 243–58.

Brown, R. E. 'Three Quotations from John the Baptist in the Gospel of John', *Catholic Biblical Quarterly*, xxii (1960), 292–8.

Brownlee, W. H. 'A Comparison of the Covenanters of the Dead Sea Scrolls with Pre-Christian Jewish Sects', *Biblical Archeologist*, xiii, 3 (1950), 69–72.

—— 'John the Baptist in the New Light of Ancient Scrolls', *Interpretation*, ix, 1 (1955), 71–90.

—— *The Meaning of the Qumrân Scrolls for the Bible* (1964).

—— 'Messianic Motifs of Qumran and the New Testament', *NTS*, iii (1956–7), 195–210.

Bultmann, R. 'Die Bedeutung des neuerschlossenen mandäischen und manichäischen Quellen für das Verständnis des Johannesevangeliums', *ZNTW*, xxiv (1925), 100–46.

Burrows, Millar. *The Dead Sea Scrolls* (1955).

Clarkson, Mary E. 'The Antecedents of the High-Priest Theme in Hebrews', *ATR*, xxix (1947), 89–95.

Cranfield, C. E. B. 'The Baptism of Our Lord—A Study of St Mark i, 9–11', *Scottish Journal of Theology*, viii, 1 (1955), 53–63.

Creed, J. M. 'Josephus on John the Baptist', *JTS*, xxiii (1922), 59–60.

Cullmann, O. *Baptism in the New Testament*, tr. by J. K. S. Reid (1950).

—— 'Die neuentdeckten Qumrân-texte und das Judenchristentum der Pseudoklementinen', *Neutestamentliche Studien für R. Bultmann* (1954), pp. 35–51.

—— 'L'Opposition contre le Temple de Jérusalem, Motif Commun de la Théologie Johannique et du Monde Ambiant', *NTS*, v, 3 (1958–9), 157–73.

—— 'The Significance of the Qumran Texts for Research into the Beginnings of Christianity', *JBL*, lxxiv (1955), 213–26.

Dahl, N. A. 'The Origin of Baptism', *Interpretationes ad Vetus Testamentum Pertinentes Sigmundo Mowinckel* (1955), pp. 36–52.

Daniélou, Jean. *Jean-Baptiste: Témoin de l'Agneau* (1964).

Darton, G. C. *St John the Baptist and the Kingdom of Heaven* (1961).

Davies, Paul E. 'Mark's Witness to Jesus', *JTS*, lxxiii (1954), 197–202.

Deane, Anthony C. 'The Ministry of John the Baptist', *The Expositor*, viii, 13 (1917), 420–31.

Del Medico, H. E. *The Riddle of the Scrolls*, tr. by H. Garner (1958).

Drews, Arthur. *The Christ Myth*, tr. by C. D. Burns (1910).

Drower, E. S. *The Canonical Prayerbook of the Mandaeans* (1959).
—— *The Secret Adam, A Study of Nasorean Gnosis* (1960).
Duncan, W. C. *The Life, Character, and Acts of John the Baptist* (1853).
Dunkerley, R. 'The Bridegroom Passage', *ET*, LXIV, 10 (1953), 303 f.
Edsman, Carl-Martin. *Le Baptême de Feu* (1940).
Enz, Jacob J. 'The Book of Exodus as a Literary Type for the Gospel of John', *JBL*, LXXVI (1957), 208–15.
Fahy, T. 'St John and Elias', *Irish Theological Quarterly*, XXIII, 3 (1956), 285 f.
Feather, J. *The Last of the Prophets* (1894).
Feuillet, A. 'Le Baptême de Jésus d'après l'Evangile selon Saint Marc', *Catholic Biblical Quarterly*, XXI (1959), 468–90.
Fitzmyer, J. A. 'The Qumran Scrolls, the Ebionites, and Their Literature', *The Scrolls and the New Testament*, ed. by K. Stendahl (1957).
Gale, Nahum. *The Prophet of the Highest: Or, The Mission of John the Baptist* (1873).
Geyser, A. S. 'The Youth of John the Baptist', *Novum Testamentum*, I (1956), 70–5.
Gnilka, J. 'Die essenischen Tauchbäder und die Johannestaufe', *RQ*, III, 2, 10 (1961), 185–207.
Grässer, Erich. *Das Problem der Parusieverzögerung in den synoptischen Evangelien und in der Apostelgeschichte* (1957).
Griffiths, D. R. 'St Matthew iii. 15...', *ET*, LXII (1950–1), 155–7.
Grobel, K. 'He That Cometh After Me', *JBL*, LX (1941), 397–401.
Guénin, Paul. *Y a-t-il eu conflit entre Jean-Baptiste et Jésus?* (1933).
Hamman, P. A. 'Le baptême par le feu', *Mélanges de Science Religieuse*, II (1951), 285–92.
Harris, J. Rendel. 'Again the Magnificat', *ET*, XLII (1930–1), 188–90.
Harrison, E. F. 'Jesus and John the Baptist', *Bibliotheca Sacra*, CII (1945), 74–83.
Heim, N. *Johannes der Verlaufer des Herrn nach Bibel, Geschichte und Tradition* (Ratisbonne, 1908).
Horne, George. *Considerations on the Life and Death of St John the Baptist* (1769).
Houghton, Ross C. *John the Baptist, the Forerunner of Our Lord: His Life and Work* (1889).
Howard, W. F. 'John the Baptist and Jesus. A Note on Evangelic Chronology', *Amicitiae Corolla: James Rendel Harris*, ed. by H. G. Wood (1933), pp. 118–32.
Innitzer, T. *Johannes der Täufer nach Schrift und Tradition* (1908).

Jack, J. W. *The Historic Christ: An Examination of Dr Robert Eisler's Theory According to the Slavonic Version of Josephus* (1933).

Jacoby, Adolf. ''Ἀνατολὴ ἐξ ὕψους', *ZNTW*, xx (1921), 205–14.

Jeremias, J. 'Proselytentaufe und Neues Testament', *Theologische Zeitschrift*, v (1949), 418–28.

—— 'Der Ursprung der Johannestaufe', *ZNTW*, xxviii (1929), 312–20.

Jones, James L. 'References to John the Baptist in the Gospel According to St Matthew', *ATR*, xli (1959), 298–302.

Jonge, M. de. 'The Testaments of the Twelve Patriarchs and the New Testament', *Studia Evangelica*, ed. by K. Aland *et al.* (1959), pp. 546–56.

Keim, Theodor. *The History of Jesus of Nazara*, vol. ii, tr. by E. M. Geldart (1876).

Kennard, J. Spencer, Jr. 'The Nazoreans' (unpublished MS), 400 pp.

—— 'The Significance of John's Break with the Essenes' (unpublished MS).

Köhler, H. *Johannes der Täufer. Kritisch-theologische Studie* (1884).

Konrad, Alois. *Johannes der Täufer* (1911).

Krieger, Norbert. 'Barfuss Busse Tun', and 'Ein Mensch in weichen Kleidern', *Novum Testamentum*, i (1956), 227–8 and 228–30 respectively.

—— 'Fiktiven Orte der Johannes-Taufe', *ZNTW*, xlv (1954), 121–3.

Leaney, A. R. C. 'The Birth Narratives in St Luke and St Matthew', *NTS*, viii, 2 (1962), 158–66.

Lightfoot, R. H. *The Gospel Message of St Mark* (1950).

Liver, J. 'The Doctrine of the Two Messiahs in Sectarian Literature in the Time of the Second Commonwealth', *HTR*, lii (1959), 149–85.

Lohmeyer, Ernst. *Lord of the Temple*, tr. by S. Todd (1961).

—— 'Von Baum und Frucht, eine exegetische Studie zu Matth. 3, 10', *Zeitschrift für Systematische Theologie*, ix (1931), 377–97.

Lohse, Eduard. 'Lukas als Theologe der Heilsgeschichte', *Evangelische Theologie*, xiv (1954), 256–75.

Lownds, F. E. 'The Baptism of Our Lord', *ET*, lxii (1950–1), 274 f.

Macgregor, G. H. C. 'Some Outstanding N.T. Problems. vii. John the Baptist and the Origins of Christianity', *ET*, xlvi (1935), 355–62.

MacNeill, H. L. 'The Sitz im Leben of Luke 1. 5–2. 20', *JBL*, lxv (1946), 123–30.

Macuch, R. 'Alter und Heimat des Mandäismus nach neuerschlossenen Quellen', *Theologische Literaturzeitung*, lxxxii (1957), 401–8.

Manson, T. W. 'John the Baptist', *Bulletin of the John Rylands Library*, xxxvi (1953–4), 395–412.

McCullagh, Archibald. *The Peerless Prophet: Or, The Life and Times of John the Baptist* (1888).

Mead, G. R. S. *The Gnostic John the Baptizer* (1924).

Meyer, F. B. *John the Baptist* (1900).

Michael, J. Hugh. 'The Sign of John', *JTS*, xxi (1919–20), 146–59.

Michaelis, W. 'Die sogenannte Johannes-Junger in Ephesus', *Neue kirchliche Zeitschrift*, xxxviii (1927), 717–36.

—— 'Täufer, Jesus, Urgemeinde', *Neutestamentliche Forschungen*, ii (1928), 16–35.

—— 'Zum jüdischen Hintergrund der Johannestaufe', *Judaica*, vii (1951), 81–120.

Morel, Robert. *L'annonciateur, vie de saint Jean le baptiste* (1942).

Morgenthaler, R. *Die lukanische Geschichtsschreibung als Zeugnis*, 2 vols. (1949).

Munk, K. 'John and Jesus', *American Scandinavian Review*, xxxii (1944), 4–9.

Parsons, E. W. 'John the Baptist and Jesus', *Studies in Early Christianity*, ed. by S. J. Case (1928).

Pick, Bernhard. 'John the Baptist and Christ in the Slavic Translation of Josephus' *Jewish War*', *The Biblical World* (N.S.), xxxiii (1914), 172–7.

Plooij, D. 'The Baptism of Jesus', *Amicitiae Corolla: James Rendel Harris*, ed. by H. G. Wood (1933), pp. 239–52.

Potter, Charles F. *The Lost Years of Jesus* (1963).

Pottgiesser, A. *Johannes der Täufer und Jesus Christus* (1911).

Preisker, H. 'Apollos und die Johannesjunger in Apg. 18–19', *ZNTW*, xxx (1931), 301–4.

Procksch, O. *Johannes der Täufer* (1907).

Reimarus, Hermann Samuel. *Fragments from Reimarus*, ed. by G. E. Lessing (1774); tr. by C. Voysey (1879).

Renan, Ernest. *Life of Jesus*, tr. from the 23rd and final edition by J. H. Allen (1903).

Reynolds, Henry Robert. *John the Baptist* (1876).

Richter, G. '"Bist du Elias?" (Joh. 1, 21)', *Biblische Zeitschrift*, vi (1962), 79–92; and vi (1962), 238–56.

Riesenfeld, H. 'La signification sacramentaire du baptême johannique', *Dieu vivant*, xiii (1949), 31–7.

—— 'Tradition und Redaktion im Markusevangelium', *Neutestamentliche Studien für R. Bultmann* (1954), pp. 157–64.

Robertson, A. T. *John the Loyal* (1911).

Robinson, Armitage. *The Historical Character of St John's Gospel* (1929).

Robinson, John A. T. 'The Baptism of John and the Qumran Community', *HTR*, L (1957), 175–91.

—— 'The Most Primitive Christology of All?', *JTS*, VII (1956), 177–89.

Rowley, H. H. 'The Baptism of John and the Qumran Sect', *New Testament Essays in Memory of T. W. Manson*, ed. by A. J. B. Higgins (1959), pp. 218–29.

—— 'Jewish Proselyte Baptism and the Baptism of John', *Hebrew Union College Annual*, XV (1940), 313–34.

—— 'The Qumran Sect and Christian Origins', *Bulletin of the John Rylands Library*, XLIV (1961), 119–56.

Sahlin, Harald. 'Die Fruchte der Umkehr', *Studia Theologica*, I (1948), 54–68.

Säve-Söderbergh, Torgny. *Studies in the Coptic Manichaean Psalm-Book* (1949).

Schäfer, Karl Th. '"... und dann werden Sie fasten an jeden Tage"', *Synoptische Studien: Alfred Wikenhauser zum siebzigsten Geburtstag* (1953).

Schmauch, Werner. 'In der Wüste', *In Memoriam Ernst Lohmeyer*, ed. by W. Schmauch (1951), pp. 202–23.

Schmitt, J. 'Les écrits du Nouveau Testament et les textes de Qumran', *Revue des Sciences Religieuses*, XXIX (1955), 394–401; XXX (1956), 55–74, 261–7.

Schnackenburg, R. 'Die Erwartung des "Propheten" nach dem Neuen Testament und den Qumran-Texten', *Studia Evangelica*, ed. by K. Aland *et al.* (1959), pp. 622–39.

Schonfield, Hugh J. *Secrets of the Dead Sea Scrolls* (1956).

Schweizer, E. 'Eine hebraisierende Sonderquelle des Lukas?', *Theologische Zeitschrift*, VI (1950), 161–85.

Seidelin, Paul. 'Das Jonaszeichen', *Studia Theologica*, V (1951), 119–31.

Silberman, Lou. 'The Two "Messiahs" of the Manual of Discipline', *Vetus Testamentum*, V (1955), 77–82.

Simon, Marcel. *Les Sectes Juives au Temps de Jésus* (1960).

Smyth, Kevin. 'St John the Baptist and the Dead Sea Scrolls', *The Month*, XX (July 1958), 352–61.

Stapfer, Edmond. *Jesus Christ Before His Ministry*, tr. by L. S. Houghton (1896).

Starr, Joshua. 'The Unjewish Character of the Markan Account of John the Baptist', *JBL*, LI (1932), 227–37.

Stauffer, Ethelbert. *Jesus and His Story*, tr. by D. M. Barton (1960).

Strange, Carl. 'Der Prolog des Johannesevangelium', *Zeitschrift für Systematische Theologie*, XXI (1950), 120–41.

Stratton, C. 'Pressure for the Kingdom', *Interpretation*, VIII (1954), 414–21.

Strecker, Georg. *Das Judenchristentum in den Pseudoklementinen* (1958).

Sutcliffe, E. F. 'Baptism and Baptismal Rites at Qumran?', *Heythrop Journal*, I (1960), 179–88.

Teeple, H. M. *The Mosaic Eschatological Prophet* (1957).

Teicher, J. L. 'The Teaching of the Pre-Pauline Church in the Dead Sea Scrolls—VI: Has a Johannine Sect Ever Existed?', *Journal of Jewish Studies*, IV (1953), 139–53.

Thompson, P. J. 'The Infancy Gospels of St Matthew and St Luke Compared', *Studia Evangelica*, ed. by K. Aland *et al.* (1959), pp. 217–22.

Vermes, G. 'Baptism and Jewish Exegesis', *NTS*, IV (1958), 308–19.

Vielhauer, Ph. 'Zum "Paulinismus" der Apostelgeschichte', *Evangelische Theologie*, X (1950–1), 1–15.

Vögtle, Anton. 'Der Spruch vom Jonaszeichen (Mk. 8, 11 f.)', *Synoptische Studien: A. Wikenhauser zum siebzigsten Geburtstag* (1953).

Volz, Paul. *Prophetengestalten des Alten Testaments* (1938).

Wagner, Siegfried. *Die Essener in der Wissenschaftlichen Diskussion vom Ausgang des 18. bis zum Beginn des 20. Jahrhunderts* (1960).

Wallace-Hadrill, D. S. 'A Suggested Exegesis of Matthew III, 9, 10 (= Luke III, 8, 9)', *ET*, LXII (1950–1), 349.

Waterman, Leroy. *Forerunners of Jesus* (1959).

Weber, Theodor. *Johannes der Täufer und die Parteien seiner Zeit* (1870).

Weed, Norman. 'John the Baptist and Jesus', unpublished Master's Thesis, Union Theological Seminary, New York (1950).

Williams, G. O. 'Baptism in Luke's Gospel', *JTS*, XLV (1944), 31–8.

Wilson, Edmund. *The Scrolls from the Dead Sea* (1955).

Wilson, R. McL. 'Some Recent Studies in the Lucan Infancy Narratives', *Studia Evangelica*, ed. by K. Aland *et al.* (1959), pp. 235–53.

Winter, Paul. 'Lc 2[49] and Targum Yerushalmi', *ZNTW*, XLV (1954), 145–79.

—— '"Nazareth" and "Jerusalem" in Luke Chs. I and II', *NTS*, III (1956–7), 136–42.

—— 'The Proto-Source of Luke I', *Novum Testamentum*, I (1956), 184–99.

Yates, J. E. 'The Form of Mark I, 8 b', *NTS*, IV (1958), 334–8.

Zurhellen, O. *Johannes der Täufer und seine Verhältnis zum Judentum* (1903).

INDEX OF PASSAGES CITED

I. OLD TESTAMENT

IV. NEW TESTAMENT APOCRYPHA

V. JEWISH TEXTS

VI. CHURCH FATHERS

INDEX OF AUTHORS

INDEX OF AUTHORS